The Publish or Perish Tutorial

80 easy tips
to get the best out of the
Publish or Perish software

Prof. Anne-Wil Harzing

Edition: September 2016

ISBN 978-0-9808485-8-8 (paperback, black & white)

Published by Tarma Software Research Ltd, London, United Kingdom.

Table of contents

Introduction

Through my technical support for Publish or Perish (PoP) over the last 10 years and the Publish or Perish Survey, I have come to realise that there is room for improvement in the way most PoP users use the program. Obviously, there are many help resources: a help file, an FAQ and the Publish or Perish book. However, most users don't seem to consult those.

Tutorial: 80 PoP tips

This tutorial of 80 tips therefore takes a different approach and introduces the user to the main functions of Publish or Perish in short and easy chunks. Most sections can be read independently, but the collection is structured in a logical order, so you can work through it doing one section at a time.

Finding out your publications, citations and h-index

We will start out with the most common usage scenario: academics searching for their own name, usually to find their publications, citations and h-index. In doing so we also discuss in detail how to disambiguate author names.

Journal search, General search, and Multi-query center

In addition to an author search, Publish or Perish also provides the option to do a journal search. For more demanding users, the general search function opens up a host of additional search options. The multi-query center stores all of your queries and allows for sophisticated query management.

From query export to job interview and much more...

Amongst many other things, you will learn about a multitude of metrics, how to manage, import and export your queries, how to use PoP to make your case for tenure or promotion, how to decide which journals to submit to, how to prepare for a job interview, how to do a literature review, and even how to do bibliometric research.

Google Scholar limitations

Although Google Scholar typically provides better coverage than Scopus or the Web of Science, it is not a bibliometric database. Instead it relies on parsing scholarly literature on the Web. Therefore, this tutorial also covers the main limitations of Google Scholar, including lack of discipline filtering, truncation of author and journal names, and the occasional wrong parsing of years, master records, author names.

Publish or Perish version 4

PoP is under continuous development. This tutorial is best suited for Publish or Perish version 4.

PoP tip 1: Author search (1): Three easy steps

Finding your own publications, citations, or h-index by using Google Scholar data can be done in three easy steps:

1. Install Publish or Perish

Download and install the Publish or Perish software on your computer. It will take less than 2 minutes and you do not need administrator rights.

2. Enter your search terms

Click on **Author Impact** in the left-hand column and enter your first initial and name in the **Authors** field.
- Use quotes around the name (e.g. "a harzing").
- It doesn't matter whether you use caps ("A Harzing" or "A HARZING") or lower case letters ("a harzing").
- The order of the search terms doesn't matter either, you can use "a harzing" or "harzing a".

3. Execute the search

Click on the button **called Lookup** [top right].

Result

That's all! If you have a lot of publications, you might need to wait up to a minute or so before PoP can retrieve all of them from Google Scholar. However, for most scholars results will show up within 1-20 seconds. The screenshot above is what my results looks like.

H-core publications

In case you are wondering..... those funny blue "h's" in front of the cites indicate that this publication is part of the set of publications that contributes to the h-index, i.e. the h-core set.

PoP tip 2: Author search (2): Do include the quotes (" ")

If searching for your own name in Publish or Perish gives you a long list of publications that are not yours, there are two possible causes.

1. You did not include quotes

You did not include quotes (e.g. "a harzing") around the name you searched for.

Why do I need to include quotes?

Google **Scholar** default search behaviour is the same as Google's default search behaviour. This means that if you do **not** use quotes around the search terms it will match your author search terms **anywhere** in the author record.

- If you do an author search without quotes, Google Scholar matches the name and initials **anywhere** in the list of authors, so P Kulik, C Williamson, would also match C Kulik.
- To match an author's initials only in combination with her or his own surname, use "quotes" around the author's name: "C Kulik" will **not** match P Kulik, C Williamson.
- However, "C Kulik" will match CT Kulik (the actual academic we are looking for), CM Kulik, NC Kulik or any other name that contains both C and Kulik. To resolve this problem, see Author disambiguation: Use multiple initials.

2. Your name is not unique

The combination of your given name and family name is not unique and there are other academics with the same name. There are many ways in which you can disambiguate your name from other academics with the same name. For more details, please see the nine following tips.

Use selective exclusion	Use full given name	Exclude co-authors
Use multiple initials	Use year restrictions	Use research field
Exclude homonyms	Use multiple names	Use affiliation

PoP tip 3: Author search (3): Use selective exclusion

If the list of results in Publish or Perish is fairly limited, the best way to disambiguate your publications from those of a namesake is selective exclusion.

Manual exclusion

You can manually exclude irrelevant publications from the analysis by checking or clearing the boxes in the Results list. Here are some shortcuts:

- The **Check all** button places check marks in all boxes;
- The **Uncheck all** button clears all boxes;
- When you use the keyboard to travel up and down in the Results list, pressing the space bar toggles the check mark on and off on the selected line.

Exclude a range of items

You can also select a consecutive range of items in the list (left-click on the first item, then hold either Shift key and left-click on the last item) and use the **Check selection / Uncheck selection** buttons to check/uncheck all selected items and recalculate the citation statistics.

Sorting by column helps with exclusions

Selecting relevant publications can be made easier by first sorting the results by **Cites**, **Authors**, **Title**, **Year**, **Publication**, or **Publisher**. Sorting is done simply by clicking on the corresponding column heading. Click twice to reverse the sort order. Sorting by author is often a very effective way to exclude a range of publications in one go as one can easily identify authors with inappropriate initials or recognize irrelevant co-authors.

Changes in results list take effect immediately

In contrast to the refinements described in other tips, changes in the Results list take effect immediately and are reflected in the summary field. You do not have to resubmit your search.

PoP tip 4: Author search (4): Use multiple initials

Another way to disambiguate authors in Publish or Perish is to use multiple initials in your search. Many academics, including nearly all US academics, have a "middle" name. Hence, you might want to use both initials when searching.

"CT Kulik" rather than "C Kulik"

For instance rather than searching for "C Kulik", you could search for "CT Kulik" instead. Usually, searching with two initials provides a very "clean" result, unless your family name is very common. Be careful though: Authors are not always consistent in the initials that they use in their publications. Even if they are, references to their articles may use other combinations or formats. It is usually safer to start your search with only one initial.

Limitations of this strategy

As an example, imagine that my family name was not unique in academia and you needed to include more than one initial to limit the search. How would you search?

- "AW Harzing" (resulting in 9079 citations)?
- "AWK Harzing" (resulting in 536 citations)?
- "AK Harzing" (resulting in 3 citations)?

As indicated in brackets, each search will give you a different result. Moreover, including my middle initial (K) is a sure-fire way to underestimate my citation impact. However, each of the three searches with more than one initial gives fewer citations than the original 9668 citations for "A Harzing" and thus underestimates my citation impact.

Google Scholar results for multiple initial search are not always intuitive

In contrast to some other sources for publication and citation data Google Scholar will provide exact matches if you search for **two or more initials**. This can be quite annoying if you search for an academic that has published some articles with two and other articles with three initials as a search with two initials will not provided the publications with three initials. If you search for one initial, this is not the case, e.g. "A Nother" will also match AB Nother" and "ABC Nother".

In the above example:

- "A Harzing" would find "A Harzing" "AW Harzing", "AWK Harzing" and "AK Harzing" and is thus the safest bet [though it would also find "AA Harzing", "AB Harzing" "AC Harzing" etc., if these people existed.]
- "AK" Harzing and "AWK Harzing" would both only find exact matches, so they will not find "AKA Harzing" or "AWKA" Harzing.
- Likewise, "AW Harzing" would only find "AW Harzing" not "AWK Harzing". Thus searching with two initials for someone who has also published with three initials will miss part of their publication record. The solution here would be to search for "AW Harzing" OR "AWK Harzing".

My recommendation

In general, this search strategy seems to be most effective with Anglophone North Americans who:

a. tend to have a middle initial, and
b. tend to use it systematically when publishing

For academics outside this group, this strategy can be a bit hit-and-miss.

PoP tip 5: Author search (5): Exclude homonyms

When searching for an author who only publishes with one initial in Publish or Perish, you can exclude academics with the same last name and first initial (but with multiple initials rather than one initial) through the use of *.

One step search for academics with a single initial

For instance Graham Sewell, one of my former Melbourne colleagues, has only published as "G Sewell". One can exclude other academics with the same last name and first initial by using "G* Sewell", "G** Sewell", "G*** Sewell" in the **Exclude these authors** field. This would exclude "GJ Sewell", "GW Sewell", "GWF Sewell" "GJTP Sewell" as well as dozens of other combinations in one go.

Author impact analysis - Perform a citation analysis for one or more authors	
Author's name:	"G Sewell"
Exclude these names:	"G* Sewell" "G** Sewell" "G*** Sewell" "EG Sewell" "RG Sewell" "Gary Sewell"
Year of publication between:	0 and: 0
Data source:	Google Scholar ▼

Limitations of this strategy

Unfortunately, you cannot use "*G Sewell" to exclude "EG Sewell" or "RG Sewell" as this excludes all names with a "G" in them, including "G Sewell", our target academic. Hence, these need to be excluded one by one, as do those with only one initial but another given name (e.g. "Gary Sewell").

Remember the quotes

Also, as before, remember to quote the exclusions. If you exclude G* Sewell, Google Scholar will interpret his as excluding both G and Sewell, thus leaving you with no results at all.

All your queries are saved for future use

You do **not** need to enter these exclusions again every time you do the same search. All your searches are automatically saved in the multi-query center. I'll tell you more about that in future tips, but you can take a peak now if you want. You will find all the queries you have ever run there.

PoP tip 6: Author search (6): Use full given name

Another possibility to limit the number of false hits in Publish or Perish, is to include the author's full given name, for instance "Carol Kulik".

Limitation of this strategy: some journals only use initials

However, this excludes any publications in which the author's given names are not spelled out in full. As journals in some fields (e.g. Operations Research) have a tendency to use initials only, for some academics this might miss many publications.

Limitation of this strategy: hyphenated names

This strategy is also likely to fail with authors with hyphenated names, as these are more likely to be reproduced incorrectly. For instance "Anne-Wil Harzing" provides 500 fewer citations than "A Harzing".

The best compromise

However, a strategy of using "initials + last name" combined with "given name + last name" might be useful if an author has mainly published with two or more initials, but has some publications with only one initial. For instance searching for "CT Kulik" OR "Carol Kulik" produces results that are identical to a broader search for "C Kulik" with a very large number of exclusions (e.g "CC Kulik" "CL Kulik" "CJ Kulik" "JC Kulik" "AC KUlik" "JA Kulik" "GC Kulik" "C** Kulik").

Author impact analysis - Perform a citation analysis for one or more authors	
Author's name:	"CT Kulik" OR "Carol Kulik"
Exclude these names:	
Year of publication between:	0 and: 0
Data source:	Google Scholar ▼

My recommendation

In general though, I would recommend only using the author's given name:

- as a last resort for authors with very common names,
- as a very "quick-and-dirty" check to see whether a particular academic has published something.

PoP tip 7: Author search (7): Use year restrictions

If you know that a certain author has only published after (or before) a certain year, you can enter the start or end years in the **Year of publication between** ... **and** ... fields Publish or Perish. This makes it much easier to disambiguate an author from a namesake from another generation.

Analyse publications for specific period

You can also use these fields if you want to analyse the author's publications from a specific period only. For instance you could look at someone's publications, citations and h-index in the last five years alone.

Author impact analysis - Perform a citation analysis for one or more authors						
Author's name:	"a harzing"					
Exclude these names:						
Year of publication between:	2011 and:	2015				
Data source:	Google Scholar ▼					

Results

Papers:	35	Papers/author:	20.62	h-index:	14	"a harzing" from 2011 to 2015: all
Citations:	707	Cites/year:	176.75	g-index:	26	Query date: 2015-12-05
Years:	4	Cites/auth/year:	114.66	hc-index:	17	Papers: 35
Cites/paper:	20.20	hI,annual:	2.75	hI,norm:	11	Citations: 707
						Years: 4

Cites		Per year	Authors	Title	Year
☑	ḣ 85	21.25	AW Harzing	Publish or Perish, version 3	2011
☑	h 84	21.00	AW Harzing, K Köste...	Babel in business: The language barrier and its solutions in the HQ-subsidia...	2011
☑	ḣ 66	33.00	AW Harzing	A preliminary test of Google Scholar as a source for citation data: a longitu...	2013
☑	h 59	19.67	AW Harzing	Journal quality list	2012
☑	h 54	13.50	S Reiche, AW Harzing	International assignments	2011
☑	h 51	25.50	AW Harzing, M Pudelko	Language competencies, policies and practices in multinational corporation...	2013
☑	ḣ 43	10.75	BS Reiche, ML Kraime...	Why do international assignees stay? An organizational embeddedn...	2011
☑	h 36	18.00	AW Harzing	Document categories in the ISI Web of Knowledge: Misunderstanding the s...	2013
☑	h 33	8.25	L Zander, AI Mockaiti...	Standardization and contextualization: A study of language and leadership...	2011
☑	h 33	16.50	H Tenzer, M Pudelko...	The impact of language barriers on trust formation in multinational teams	2013
☑	h 28	14.00	AW Harzing, BS Reic...	Challenges in international survey research: a review with illustrations and ...	2013
☑	h 23	23.00	AW Harzing	A longitudinal study of Google Scholar coverage between 2012 and 2013	2014
☑	ḣ 19	6.33	AW Harzing, K Köste...	Response style differences in cross-national research	2012
☑	h 18	9.00	AW Harzing	Practicing what we preach	2013

Careful: Sometimes Google Scholar does not parse the year

In some cases Google Scholar's parsing does not include the year of publication in the cited work. This means that if you restrict the years of publication, this work will not always show up (as there is no year field). Although Google Scholar is constantly improving these parsing errors, for important searches it is safer to quickly re-run the analysis without the year restrictions and check whether there are any highly cited works without a year indication in the results.

Your notes

PoP tip 8: Author search (8): Use multiple names

You can use the logical **OR** operator in the author field in Publish or Perish to find articles written by a range of authors. This strategy is very useful if you are searching for an author who has published under different names as it allows you to get a complete record for this author.

Maiden name and married name

The most frequent reason for this is women publishing under their maiden and married name or under different married names.

For instance Rebecca Piekkari started out publishing as Rebecca Marschan in 1996, adopted Rebecca Marschan-Piekkari in 1998, before finally settling on Rebecca Piekkari in 2005.

Author impact analysis - Perform a citation analysis for one or more authors

Author's name:	"R Marschan" OR "R Marschan-Piekkari" OR "R Piekkari"
Exclude these names:	
Year of publication between:	and:
Data source:	Google Scholar

Results

Papers:	162	Papers/author:	68.49	h-index:	29	"R Marschan" OR "R Marschan-Piekkari" OR "R Piekkari": all
Citations:	4173	Cites/year:	198.71	g-index:	63	Query date: 2015-12-05
Years:	21	Cites/auth/year:	76.98	hc-index:	26	Papers: 162
Cites/paper:	25.76	hI,annual:	1.05	hI,norm:	22	Citations: 4173
						Years: 21

Cites		Per year	Authors	Title	Year
✓ h	394	35.82	R Marschan-Piekkari, C Welch	Qualitative research methods in international business: The state of the...	2004
✓ h	342	21.38	R Marschan-Piekkari, D Welch, L Welch	In the shadow: The impact of language on structure, power and commu...	1999
✓ h	262	14.56	R Marschan, D Welch, L Welch	Language: The forgotten factor in multinational management	1997
✓ h	250	62.50	C Welch, R Piekkari, E Plakoyiannaki...	Theorising from case studies: Towards a pluralist future for internationa...	2011
✓ h	201	20.10	E Vaara, J Tienari, R Piekkari...	Language and the circuits of power in a merging multinational corporation	2005
✓ h	198	28.29	R Piekkari, C Welch, E Paavilainen	The case study as disciplinary convention: Evidence from international ...	2008
✓ h	187	14.38	C Welch, R Marschan-Piekkari, H Pe...	Corporate elites as informants in qualitative international business rese...	2002
✓ h	175	10.94	R Marschan-Piekkari, D Welch...	Adopting a common corporate language: IHRM implications	1999
✓ h	156	12.00	M Charles, R Marschan-Piekkari	Language training for enhanced horizontal communication: A challenge ...	2002
✓ h	145	18.13	K Makela, HK Kalla, R Piekkari	Interpersonal similarity as a driver of knowledge sharing within multinati...	2007

Analyse co-author pairs

You can also use this feature to analyse co-author pairs. To search for articles co-written by specific authors, enter all their names in the **Author's name** field. There is no need to add AND.

For instance: "A Harzing" "M Pudelko" will return only articles that have both authors in their author list. As you can see below, Markus and I have published 13 papers together in the last nine years.

Author's name: "a harzing" "m pudelko"

Exclude these names:

Year of publication between: and:

Data source: Google Scholar

Results

Papers:	13	Papers/author:	5.67	h-index:	8	"a harzing" "m pudelko": all
Citations:	385	Cites/year:	48.13	g-index:	13	Query date: 2015-12-05
Years:	8	Cites/auth/year:	22.66	hc-index:	8	Papers: 13
Cites/paper:	29.62	hI,annual:	0.75	hI,norm:	6	Citations: 385 Years: 8

Cites		Per year	Authors	Title	Year	Publication
✓ h	183	22.88	M Pudelko, AW Harzing	Country-of-origin, localization, or dominance effect? An empirical inves…	2007	Human Resource Management
✓ h	51	25.50	AW Harzing, M Pudelko	Language competencies, policies and practices in multinational corporati…	2013	Journal of World Business
✓ h	39	5.57	M Pudelko, AW Harzing	The Golden Triangle for MNCs:: Standardization Towards Headquarters …	2008	Organizational dynamics
✓ h	33	16.50	H Tenzer, M Pudelko…	The impact of language barriers on trust formation in multinational teams	2013	Journal of International …
✓ h	28	14.00	…, BS Reiche, M Pud…	Challenges in international survey research: a review with illustrations a…	2013	European Journal of …
✓ h	18	2.25	M Pudelko, AW Harzing	How European is management in Europe? An analysis of past, present …	2007	European Journal of International …
✓ h	12	12.00	AW Harzing, M Pudelko	Hablas vielleicht un peu la mia language? A comprehensive overview of …	2014	The International Journal of Human …
✓ h	10	1.25	M Pudelko, AW Harzing	HRM practices in subsidiaries of US, Japanese and German MNCs: Coun…	2007	Human Resource Management
✓	5	1.00	M Pudelko, AW Harzing	3 Japanese human resource management	2010	Challenges of Human Resource …
✓	3	3.00	S Reiche, AW Harzin…	Why and how does shared language affect subsidiary knowledge inflow…	2015	Journal of International …
✓	2	2.00	AW Harzing, M Pudel…	The bridging role of expatriates and inpatriates in knowledge transfer in…	2015	Human Resource …
✓	1	1.00	M Pudelko, H Tenzer,…	Cross-cultural management and language studies within international b…	2014	Routledge companion to …
✓	0	0.00	AW Harzing, M Pudelko	Do we need to distance ourselves from the distance concept? Why hom…	2015	Management International Review

PoP tip 9: Author search (9): Exclude co-authors

How do you disambiguate in Publish or Perish if you are unlucky enough to have a name-sake with exactly the same family name and given name and no second initial to differentiate? There are many Peter Smiths or Michelle Browns!

Use co-authors to disambiguate

If you are lucky, your namesake has published with only a limited number of co-authors. In that case, you can use the name of **other** co-authors to restrict the search. You will probably need to combine multiple search strategies described above.

Extended example: Michelle Brown

Let's take Michelle Brown, a former colleague of mine at the University of Melbourne working in industrial relations and human resource management, as an example. Looking for "M Brown" alone gets us nowhere, there are more than 1,000 results. That doesn't even include all of Michelle's own papers. Google Scholar limits the results to the 1,000 most cited papers and even the least cited result still had 53 citations. Hence many papers with fewer citations are not reported.

- Using Michelle Brown instead of "M Brown" (Use full given name) already limits the number results to 614 and lists all of Michelle's papers.
- Excluding "M* Brown" and "M** Brown" (Exclude homonyms) brings the results down to 357.
- Excluding "AM Brown" "BM Brown" "CM Brown" "JM Brown" "KM Brown" "LM Brown" "TM Brown" and limiting the starting year to 1997 (Use year restrictions) brings the results further down to 252.
- Excluding co-authors "F Princen" "F Wilson" "G Studer" "K Kendall" "CL Gardner" "B Sourkes" "B Hoffman" brings us down to 227.

Limitations of this strategy

Unfortunately, Google Scholar only allows a certain number of characters in the **Exclude these authors** field and we have now run out. As the screenshot below shows, we are still not there as the first four publications are not Michelle's. Still, there are now only just over 200 publications to go through manually instead of 1,000.

Workable strategy if you need h-index only

Moreover, if you are only interested in the h-index there are now only about 30 publications to check (of which 17 are Michelle's). As all the "offending" publications are in Medicine, History, or Media Studies this should be fairly easy.

All your queries are saved for future use

You do not need to enter these exclusions again every time you do the same search. All your searches are automatically saved in the multi-query center. I'll tell you more about that in future tips, but you can take a peak now if you want. You will find all the queries you have ever run there.

15

PoP tip 10: Author search (10): Use research fields

We left Michelle Brown [see Exclude co-authors] with just over 200 publications, of which I know – since I am familiar with her publication record – about three quarters are not hers. So unless we are only interested in her h-index, this still leaves us with quite a lot of manual verification.

Use inclusions instead of exclusions

Hence another strategy is to start at the other end and work with **inclusions** rather than exclusions. For this we need the Publish or Perish **General citation search** function. This function has all of the fields that the author search has, but also provides the opportunity to enter keywords that either need to be included or excluded.

Extended example: enter two research fields

Michelle works in industrial relations and human resource management. So what happens if we simply include these two research fields in **any of the words**? Hey presto, this provides us with more than 95% of Michelle's actual citations and provides a correct h-index.

General citation search - Perform a general citation search					
Author(s):	"Michelle Brown"				
Publication:					
All of the words:					
Any of the words:	"industrial relations" "human resource management"				
None of the words:					
The phrase:					
Year of publication between:	1997 and: 0	Title words only			
Data source:	Google Scholar				

Results

Papers:	52	Papers/author:	24.65	h-index:	17	"Michelle Brown", "industrial relations" "human resource management" from 1997: all
Citations:	1232	Cites/year:	68.44	g-index:	35	Query date: 2015-12-05
Years:	18	Cites/auth/year:	32.28	hc-index:	14	Papers: 52 Citations: 1232
Cites/paper:	23.69	hI,annual:	0.72	hI,norm:	13	Years: 18

Cites	Per year	Rank	Authors	Title
h 138	12.55	4	J Barry Hocking, M Brown	A knowledge transfer perspective of strategic assignment purposes and their path-dependent outcomes
h 129	12.90	1	M Brown, JS Heywood	Performance appraisal systems: determinants and change
h 111	15.86	2	M Brown, C Cregan	Organizational change cynicism: The role of employee involvement
h 90	11.25	5	JB Hocking, M Brown	Balancing global and local strategic contexts: Expatriate knowledge transfer, applications, and learning wi
h 90	11.25	15	J Benson, M Brown	Knowledge workers: what keeps them committed; what turns them away
h 86	17.20	16	M Brown, D Hyatt, J Benson	Consequences of the performance appraisal experience
h 80	20.00	7	J Benson, M Brown	Generations at work: are there differences and do they matter?
h 71	5.92	6	M Brown, J Benson	Rated to exhaustion? Reactions to performance appraisal processes
h 65	6.50	18	M Brown, J Benson	Managing to overload? Work overload and performance appraisal processes
h 65	4.64	47	M Brown	Unequal pay, unequal responses? Pay referents and their implications for pay level satisfaction
h 49	6.13	51	P Kavanagh, J Benson, M B...	Understanding performance appraisal fairness
h 32	5.33	3	M Brown, I Metz, C Cregan	Irreconcilable differences? Strategic human resource management and employee well-being
h 25	3.13	25	M Brown, LA Geddes, JS He...	The determinants of employee-involvement schemes: private sector Australian evidence
h 24	1.71	9	M Brown	Merit pay preferences among public sector employees
h 21	4.20	10	J Benson, M Brown	Employee voice: does union membership matter?
h 17	1.00	8	S Bertone, M Brown, P Cres...	Developing effective consultative practices: case studies of consultation at work
h 17	2.83	11	CT Kulik, C Cregan, I Metz, ...	HR managers as toxin handlers: The buffering effect of formalizing toxin handling responsibilities

Use "any of the words" rather than "all of the words"

Make sure you use **any of the words** not **all of the words**. Otherwise only articles that include both sets of words would be included.

Limitations of this strategy

Google Scholar is **not** a bibliometric database like the Web of Science or Scopus. Google Scholar only has fields for authors, title, source and year. It does not have dedicated fields for research area or affiliation. Hence, if you do a keyword search with research areas Google Scholar will match those **anywhere** in the document. This means that you might still get inappropriate results, if for instance the research area occurs in one of the references, even though the article is in another field.

All your queries are saved for future use

You do **not** need to enter these inclusions again every time you do the same search. All your searches are automatically saved in the multi-query center. I'll tell you more about that in future tips, but you can take a peak now if you want. You will find all the queries you have ever run there.

PoP tip 11: Author search (11): Use affiliation

As an alternative to research fields [Use research fields], you can also try university affiliations to disambiguate your own publication record from namesakes in Publish or Perish. This is particularly effective if you have only worked in a limited number of places.

Extended example: Prakash Singh

For instance, another of my former colleagues at Melbourne – Prakash Singh – is also a nightmare to search for as both Prakash and Singh are very common names for ethnic Indians. "P Singh" and "Prakash Singh" both provide more than 1,000 results, even though my colleague only has about 70-80 publications.

Fortunately, he had published most of his work as "PJ Singh", but even that search provided more than 400 results and missed a couple of his publications as "Prakash Singh". So the solution was to use the **General citation search** for "PJ Singh" OR "Prakash Singh", but restricting it by university affiliation, as I knew Prakash had only published with two affiliations: "University of Melbourne" and "Monash University".

General citation search - Perform a general citation search

Author(s):	"Prakash Singh" OR "PJ Singh"
Publication:	
All of the words:	
Any of the words:	"university of melbourne" "monash university" "supply chain"
None of the words:	"RP Singh" "S Prakash Singh" "SP Singh" hip
The phrase:	
Year of publication between:	and: 0 ☐ Title words only
Data source:	Google Scholar

Results

Papers:	78	Papers/author:	33.08	h-index:	16	"Prakash Singh" OR "PJ Singh", "university of melbourne" "monash university" "supply chain",
Citations:	1459	Cites/year:	112.23	g-index:	38	Query date: 2015-12-05
Years:	13	Cites/auth/year:	44.45	hc-index:	15	Papers: 78
Cites/paper:	18.71	hI,annual:	0.85	hI,norm:	11	Citations: 1459
						Years: 13

Cites		Per year	Rank	Authors	Title
☑ h	446	49.56	1	, B Squire, K Burgess, PJ Singh...	Supply chain management: a structured literature review and implications for future research
☑ h	148	13.45	4	PJ Singh, AJR Smith	Relationship between TQM and innovation: an empirical study
☑ h	99	14.14	41	PJ Singh	Empirical assessment of ISO 9000 related management practices and performance relationship
☑ h	97	10.78	47	PJ Singh, M Feng, A Smith	ISO 9000 series of standards: comparison of manufacturing and service organisations
☑ h	95	10.56	59	B Bernstein, PJ Singh	An integrated innovation process model based on practices of Australian biotechnology firms
☑ h	90	15.00	2	PJ Singh, D Power	The nature and effectiveness of collaboration between firms, their customers and suppliers: a
☑ h	61	15.25	63	PJ Singh, D Power, SC Chuong	A resource dependence theory perspective of ISO 9000 in managing organizational environmen
☑ h	53	5.89	5	K Burgess, PJ Singh	A proposed integrated framework for analysing supply chains
☑ h	46	4.60	3	PJ Singh, A Smith, AS Sohal*	Strategic supply chain management issues in the automotive industry: an Australian perspectiv
☑ h	46	5.11	43	PJ Singh, P Mansour-Nahra	ISO 9000 in the public sector: a successful case from Australia
☑ h	43	5.38	37	D Power, P Singh	The e-integration dilemma: the linkages between internet technology application, trading partn
☑ h	42	4.67	8	F Franceschini, M Galetto, PJ Singh...	An empirically validated quality management measurement instrument
☑ h	22	3.14	72	B Bernstein, PJ Singh	Innovation generation process: Applying the adopter categorization model and concept of "cha
☑ h	21	7.00	11	V Bhakoo, P Singh, A Sohal	Collaborative management of inventory in Australian hospital supply chains: practices and issue
☑ h	21	2.33	61	PJ Singh, A Smith	Uncovering the faultlines in quality management
☑ h	16	4.00	9	..., CJ Anumba, TR Lee, J Wang, PJ Sin...	Sourcing from China: experiences of Australian firms

Further fine-tuning the search

This search indeed provided more than 95% of his citations, but missed one publication with 46 citations that would have increased his h-index by 1. However, when I added "supply chain" (his main research area) as another keyword this publication appeared. This did introduce a couple of publications by "S Prakash Singh", "SP Singh" and "RP Singh"; hence these names were entered in "none of the words". We also included the word "hip" to remove a couple of lowly cited publications by another "PJ Singh", although they did not influence the metrics much.

The result (see above) was a very comprehensive list of Prakash's publications with only three inclusions and four exclusions. Make sure you use **any of the words** not **all of the words**. Otherwise only articles that include both sets of words would be included.

Limitations of this strategy

Obviously you do need to know a little bit about the person you are searching for in order to be able to come up with smart inclusions. However, if you are searching for your own name, that should not be a problem. Google Scholar is **not** a bibliometric database like the Web of Science or Scopus. Google Scholar only has fields for authors, title, source and year. It does not have dedicated fields for research area or affiliation. Hence, if you do a keyword search with affiliation Google Scholar will match this **anywhere** in the document. This means that you might still get inappropriate results, where for instance the affiliation occurs in one of the references even though the academic has no connection with it.

All your queries are saved for future use

You do **not** need to enter these inclusions and exclusions again every time you do the same search. All your searches are automatically saved in the multi-query center. I'll tell you more about that in future tips, but you can take a peak now if you want. You will find all the queries you have ever run there.

PoP tip 12: Journal search (1): Basic Search

The Publish or Perish Journal impact analysis page allows you to perform an analysis of the impact of a journal's publications. This page contains a query pane with the minimum parameters that are necessary to look up the journal's publications on Google Scholar in three easy steps.

1. Install Publish or Perish

Download and install the Publish or Perish software on your computer. It will take less than 2 minutes and you do not need administrator rights.

2. Enter your search terms

Click on **Journal Impact** in the left-hand column and enter the "journal's name" in the **journal title** field.

- Use quotes around the name (e.g. "Management International Review").
- It doesn't matter whether you use caps ("Management International Review" or "MANAGEMENT INTERNATIONAL REVIEW") or lower case letters ("management international review").

3. Execute the search

Click on the button called "lookup" [top right].

Result

A search like this provides good results for journals with fairly unique names such as *"Management International Review"* or *"International Journal of Cross Cultural Management"*.

Journal impact analysis - Perform a citation analysis for one or more journals

Journal title:	"Management International Review"
Exclude these words:	
Year of publication between:	0 and: 0
Data source:	Google Scholar

Results

Papers:	1000	Cites/paper:	21.03	h-index:	67	"Management International Review": all
Citations:	21025	Cites/author:	13279.37	g-index:	110	Query date: 2015-12-12
Years:	49	Papers/author:	736.38	hI,norm:	50	Papers: 1000 Citations: 21025
Cites/year:	429.08	Authors/paper:	1.66	hI,annual:	1.02	Years: 49

Cites		Per year	Authors	Title	Year	Publication
☑ h	551	20.41	B Kogut	A study of the life cycle of joint ventures	1988	Management International Review
☑ h	420	16.15	JD Daniels, J Bracker	Profit performance: do foreign operations make a differen...	1989	Management International Review
☑ h	400	16.00	HW Lane, PW Beamish	Cross-cultural cooperative behavior in joint ventures in LDCs	1990	Management International Review
☑ h	386	42.89	J Johanson, JE Vahlne	Commitment and opportunity development in the internati...	2006	Management International Review
☑ h	282	10.07	FN Burton, BB Schlegel...	Profile analyses of non-exporters versus exporters group...	1987	Management International Review
☑ h	269	8.68	E Dichtl, M Leibold, HG...	The export-decision of small and medium-sized firms: A re...	1984	Management International
☑ h	251	31.38	DB Minbaeva	Knowledge transfer in multinational corporations	2007	Management International Review
☑ h	244	7.87	E Kaynak, V Kothari	Export behaviour of small and medium-sized manufacturer...	1984	Management International Review
☑ h	243	8.68	PW Beamish	Joint ventures in LDCs: Partner selection and performance	1987	Management International Review
☑ h	230	6.57	S Rabino	An examination of barriers to exporting encountered by s...	1980	Management International Review
☑ h	226	7.79	BL Kedia, J Chhokar	Factors inhibiting export performance of firms: an empiric...	1986	Management International Review
☑ h	226	28.25	JF Hennart	The theoretical rationale for a multinationality-performanc...	2007	Management International Review
☑ h	201	12.56	C Brewster	Strategic human resource management: the value of diffe...	1999	Management International Review

PoP tip 13: Journal search (2): Excluding journal namesakes by journal name or keywords

Just like individuals, journals sometimes have very common names, leading to Publish or Perish results that are not all related to the journal you are searching for.

Search for generic journal name gets many irrelevant results

Searching for "*Journal of Management*" will also get you:

- Journals with prefixes before "*Journal of ...* " such as Australian / British / European / Scandinavian / Sri Lankan Journal of Management
- Journals with additional words after "*Journal of Management*" such as Development / Education / Studies / Information Studies / in Engineering

Exclude journals by exclude these words

You can attempt to exclude these journals by entering them into the **exclude these words** field. This strategy needs to be applied with extreme care, however, as Google Scholar matches **exclude these words** anywhere in the papers (including the list of references for those publications that have full-text online access).

Be careful: you might exclude too much

Hence if you simply exclude "British" you will exclude any article that has the word British anywhere in its abstract, text, or references, which is clearly not the intention. Likewise if you exclude "Education", "Development" or even "Management Education" and "Management Development", any articles in the *Journal of Management* containing those words will be excluded.

Even very specific exclusions might not be entirely safe

Even excluding "*British Journal of Management*" is not entirely safe as it will exclude articles in the *Journal of Management* that refer to this journal in their list of references, a not un-likely occurrence. Therefore, this strategy will only work if you exclude journals that are in a very different field such as for instance "*Journal of Management in Engineering*".

Exclude these names works broadly

Unfortunately, unlike for the author search [Author search: Exclude homonyms], it is not possible to ensure Google Scholar excludes names only in the journal title field. Google Scholar does not seem to have implemented this feature.

PoP tip 14: Journal search (3): Excluding journal namesakes by ISSN

Just like individuals journals sometimes have very common names. If excluding journal namesakes by title (Journal search: Exclude homonyms) is not feasible in Publish or Perish, a good option is to exclude journals by ISSN.

Excluding JoM namesakes by ISSN

Taking the *Journal of Management* as an example, a search for 1990 presents us with 483 results, which includes a dozen journals that have "*Journal of Management*" as part of their name, such as "*British Journal of Management*" or "*Journal of Management Development*". However, we can exclude all these hits by excluding the ISSN numbers for these journals (see screenshot).

ISSN exclusion is a safer option

The advantage of using ISSN exclusion over excluding by journal name is that this does not accidentally remove full-text articles from the *Journal of Management* that include references with one of these journal titles.

ISSN exclusion does not exclude stray citations

The disadvantage is that using ISSN exclusion does not exclude the slightly "dubious" results with a [citation] preface. These are results to which Google Scholar found references, but for which the original work was not found online. The reason is that Google Scholar is unable to find the ISSN number in the data that it does have access to.

Use "uncheck citation" to remove stray citations

However, this is easily resolved by clicking the button **Uncheck CITATION**. Unchecking [citation] records is not recommended for an author impact search as many books, book chapters, and other non-traditional publications (such as software) are of this type. Hence removing these results would disadvantage authors who publish (some of) their work in these outlets.

For a journal impact search these results typically do not seem to add much. Hence it is generally safe to exclude these hits. This leaves us with exactly 64 results for *Journal of Management*, a number that is identical to the result of a Web of Science search for this journal for 1990.

PoP tip 15: Journal search (4): Excluding journal namesakes by ISSN: a quick-and-dirty strategy

Journal titles that include very common words present additional difficulties.

Google Scholar matches "published in" for both the publication and publisher field

The Publish or Perish journal impact analysis uses the Google Scholar Advanced query "return articles published in". Google Scholar interprets this query broadly and returns matches for both the publication and the publisher.

Generic journal title leads to many false matches

This means that a search for a relatively generic journal title such as *Information Systems Research* might get additional matches in the publisher field, such as Center for Information Systems Research. It will even report results for the eventual co-sponsor/co-publisher of *MIS Quarterly* (Management Information Systems Research Center, University of Minnesota), even though this is not directly visible in the Google Scholar output.

More results for another journal than for the target journal

As a result, most hits for a citation analysis for the journal *Information Systems Research* would be papers published in *MIS Quarterly*. Papers in this journal on average tend to be more highly cited than papers in *Information Systems Research* and hence end up more highly in the search ranking.

Excludes these words cannot be safely used

Including *MIS Quarterly* in the **Exclude these words** field is not an option, because Google Scholar matches the exclusion words anywhere in the paper. This would therefore also exclude any papers in *Information Systems Research* that are available full text and merely refer to papers published in MIS, a not unlikely occurrence.

Two strategies to get accurate results

One of the two following strategies is recommended to calculate the citation impact in this and similar cases:

Strategy 1: manual exclusions

1. Search for *Information Systems Research* without any exclusions.

2. Sort the results by Publication.

3. Unselect all papers.

4. Manually select all papers published in Information Systems Research and click Check selection.

This is probably the fastest option, but might not provide completely accurate results if there are a lot of false hits. Since Google Scholar limits the total number of results to 1000, the false hits might suppress some papers of the journal of interest that are not as highly cited. This is most likely to be a problem in disciplines where papers are generally highly cited (e.g. medicine), but it might make a difference for other fields as well.

Strategy 2: excluding by ISSN

The second strategy safely eliminates false hits and provides a more accurate result:

1. Search for *Information Systems Research*, but include the ISSN of MIS Quarterly (0276-7783) in the **Exclude these words** field. This prevents Google Scholar from excluding all ISR papers that include a MISQ reference in their list of references, but still excludes the many MIS Quarterly hits.

2. Additional exclusions are possible, as long as they are unique enough to not be likely to appear anywhere in papers published in ISR.

3. Sort the results by Publication.

4. Unselect all papers.

5. Manually select all papers published in *Information Systems Research* and click **Check selection**.

PoP tip 16: Journal search (5): Searching by ISSN

Rather than **excluding** journals by ISSN we can also **search** for journals by ISSN in Publish or Perish. This strategy gives a fairly good result for most journals.

Searching by ISSN provides "clean" results

The advantage is that searching by ISSN tends to limit results to hits coming from the publisher's official website, thus automatically removing the more dubious stray citations from other sources.

ISSN searching works if publishers structure their websites appropriately

However, this strategy is only successful if the publisher has structured their website sufficiently well for Google Scholar to parse their ISSN. Fortunately, most journals seem to be improving their websites in this respect. For instance, whereas in 2010 a search for *Australian Journal of Management* by ISSN provided no results, it now provides a comprehensive set of articles (see screenshot).

Journal impact analysis – Perform a citation analysis for one or more journals

Journal title: "Australian Journal of Management"

Journal ISSN: 1327-2020

Exclude these words:

Year of publication between: 2005 and: 0

Data source: Google Scholar

Results

Papers:	269	Cites/paper:	10.95	h-index:	27	"Australian Journal of Management", 1327-2020 from 2005: all	
Citations:	2946	Cites/author:	1529.44	g-index:	42	Query date: 2015-12-24	
Years:	10	Papers/author:	144.37	hI,norm:	18	Papers: 269 Citations: 2946	
Cites/year:	294.60	Authors/paper:	2.36	hI,annual:	1.80	Years: 10	

Cites	Authors	Title	Year	Publication	Publisher
✓ h 114	JC Sarros, J Gra...	The organizational culture profile revisited and rev...	2005	Journal of Management	aum.sagepub.com
✓ h 114	S Akhtar	The determinants of capital structure for Australia...	2005	Australian journal of management	aum.sagepub.com
✓ h 103	JS Choi, YM Kwa...	Corporate social responsibility and corporate finan...	2010	Australian Journal of Management	aum.sagepub.com
✓ h 103	P Tharenou	Does mentor support increase women's career ad...	2005	Australian Journal of Management	aum.sagepub.com
✓ h 81	P Gharghori, H C...	Are the Fama-French factors proxying default risk?	2007	Journal of Management	aum.sagepub.com
✓ h 78	M Grimmer, M Oddy	Violation of the psychological contract: The mediat...	2007	Australian Journal of Management	aum.sagepub.com
✓ h 72	JL Birt, CM Bilson...	Ownership, competition, and financial disclosure	2006	Journal of Management	aum.sagepub.com
✓ h 71	W Guay, SP Koth...	Properties of implied cost of capital using analysts'...	2011	Australian Journal of Management	aum.sagepub.com
✓ h 52	M Chang, G D'An...	Does disclosure quality via investor relations affec...	2008	Journal of management	aum.sagepub.com
✓ h 52	S Gray, A Mirkovi...	The determinants of credit ratings: Australian evid...	2006	Journal of Management	aum.sagepub.com
✓ h 46	EL Schultz, DT T...	Endogeneity and the corporate governance-perfo...	2010	journal of Management	aum.sagepub.com
✓ h 46	HWH Chan, RW ...	Fund size, transaction costs and performance: Siz...	2009	Journal of Management	aum.sagepub.com
✓ h 45	K Chalmers, G Cli...	Changes in value relevance of accounting informa...	2011	Journal of Management	aum.sagepub.com
✓ h 45	PK Pham, JA Suc...	Corporate governance and alternative performan...	2011	Journal of Management	aum.sagepub.com
✓ h 44	P Brewewer	Psychic distance and Australian export market sel...	2007	Australian Journal of Management	aum.sagepub.com
✓ h 44	RB Durand, M Li...	Momentum in Australia—a note	2006	Journal of Management	aum.sagepub.com
✓ h 43	LC Chi, TC Tang	Bankruptcy prediction: application of logit analysis...	2006	Australian Journal of Management	aum.sagepub.com
✓ h 41	AW Harzing	Australian research output in economics and busin...	2005	Australian Journal of Management	aum.sagepub.com

Combine journal name and ISSN for the best results

My experiments suggest that the best results are acquired by combining journal name and ISSN, but as Google Scholar is not constructed as a bibliographic database I cannot give any guarantees that this is true for all journals.

My recommendations

Hence my recommendations are as follows:

- If your only aim were to get a "quick and dirty" overview of the type of articles a journal publishes, I would recommend using ISSN and journal title or simply ISSN alone.
- If a comprehensive and accurate result is needed, my suggestion would be to run a couple of trial searches with name, ISSN and a combination of the two to establish what provides the best result.

PoP tip 17: Journal search (6): Year restrictions

If you would like to analyse the impact of a journal over a specific period, you can enter the start or end years in the **Year of publication between** ... **and** ... fields in Publish or Perish.

Study journal metrics for the last 3 or the last 5 years

For instance you could look at a journal's publications, citations and h-index in the last three or five years alone. Below for instance you will find the results for the last three years of the *Journal of International Business Studies*.

Journal impact analysis - Perform a citation analysis for one or more journals

Journal title: "Journal of International Business Studies"

Exclude these words:

Year of publication between: 2013 and: 2015

Data source: Google Scholar

Results

Papers:	188	Cites/paper:	9.18	h-index:	20	"Journal of International Business Studies" from
Citations:	1726	Cites/author:	850.53	g-index:	29	Query date: 2015-12-13
Years:	2	Papers/author:	89.80	hI,norm:	13	Papers: 188
Cites/year:	863.00	Authors/paper:	2.54	hI,annual:	6.50	Citations: 1726
						Years: 2

Cites		Per year	Authors	Title	Year
☑ *h*	74	74.00	DJ Teece	A dynamic capabilities-based entrepreneurial theory of th...	2014
☑ *h*	52	26.00	S Beugelsdijk, R Mudambi	MNEs as border-crossing multi-location enterprises: The ro...	2013
☑ *h*	51	25.50	E Autio, S Pathak, K Wennberg	Consequences of cultural practices for entrepreneurial be...	2013
☑ *h*	45	22.50	KD Brouthers	A retrospective on: Institutional, cultural and transaction ...	2013
☑ *h*	41	20.50	ER Banalieva, C Dhanaraj	Home-region orientation in international expansion strate...	2013
☑ *h*	41	20.50	S Ronen, O Shenkar	Mapping world cultures: Cluster formation, sources and im...	2013
☑ *h*	40	20.00	X Ma, TW Tong, M Fitza	How much does subnational region matter to foreign subsi...	2013
☑ *h*	37	18.50	JM Shaver	Do we really need more entry mode studies&quest	2013
☑ *h*	36	18.00	A Goerzen, CG Asmussen...	Global cities and multinational enterprise location strategy	2013
☑ *h*	34	17.00	H Tenzer, M Pudelko...	The impact of language barriers on trust formation in multi...	2013
☑ *h*	32	16.00	N Boubakri, SA Mansi, W Saffar	Political institutions, connectedness, and corporate risk-ta...	2013

Online publication year vs. print publication year

However, here a problem arises. Sometimes, though by no means always, Google Scholar will parse the year in which a paper was put online before being assigned to a print issue. [Google Scholar: inconsistent year] For instance the article highlighted above was published in 2014, but is listed as a 2013 publication as it was published in online first on the 19th of December 2013.

The impact of language barriers on trust formation in multinational teams

Helene Tenzer, Markus Pudelko & Anne-Wil Harzing

Affiliations | Corresponding author

Journal of International Business Studies (2014) **45**, 508–535 | doi:10.1057/jibs.2013.64
Received 13 November 2012 | Revised 26 September 2013 | Accepted 16 October 2013 |
Published online 19 December 2013

Online first publication might disturb results for a specific year

This is not a problem if you look at journal impact for a number of years, but it is a problem if you want to include only one specific year. It is also problematic for authors wanting to compare their citation scores to other articles published the same year. [Google Scholar: inconsistent year]

PoP tip 18: Journal search (7): Searching chapters in an edited volume

Although journals are the most common sources of publications, the Publish or Perish Journal Impact search can also be used to search for publications in other sources. Edited book volumes are a common source in the Social Sciences and Humanities.

Comprehensive citation counts for edited volumes

Typically a lot of authors will refer to individual chapters within an edited book. Hence, in order to assess the overall impact of an edited book, one would need to search for citations to individual chapters as well as citations to the book as a whole.

1. The easiest way to search for citations to the book *as a whole* is to search for the editor(s) of the book and include the year of publication.
2. To find citations of chapters that appear in an edited volume, use these parameters:
   - **Journal title**: enter the title of the edited volume, preferably within quotes.
   - **Year of publication between ... and ...**: enter the copyright year of the volume in both fields.
   - Depending on the number of matches that you find, you may want to use the **Exclude these words** field to restrict the search.

Worked Example: Handbook of organization studies

In 1996 Cynthia Hardy, Stewart Clegg and Walter Nord published the *Handbook of Organization Studies*. A new edition of this book appeared in 2006. If we want to establish the impact that this handbook has had on the field, we need to be able to accumulate citations to all chapters in this handbook.

Searching for the editors using multiple author names

When searching for the editors, I found a total of 1115 citations to the Handbook as such. As described in [Author disambiguation: Use multiple names], this can be done easily by including the three family names in the authors name field. Google Scholar then only provides publications co-written by these three authors.

Author impact analysis - Perform a citation analysis for one or more authors

Author's name: hardy clegg nord

Exclude these authors:

Year of publication between: 0 and: 0

Data source: Google Scholar

Results

Papers:	36	Cites/paper:	35.19	h-index:	8	hardy clegg nord: all	
Citations:	1267	Cites/author:	332.62	g-index:	35	Query date: 2015-12-13	
Years:	19	Papers/author:	9.90	hI,norm:	4	Papers: 36	
Cites/year:	66.68	Authors/paper:	3.83	hI,annual:	0.21	Citations: 1267 Years: 19	

Cites		Per year	Authors	Title
☑ *h*	946	105.11	SR Clegg, C Hardy, T Lawrence, WR Nord	The Sage handbook of organization studies
☑ *h*	169	9.94	SR Clegg, C Hardy, WR Nord	Handbook de estudos organizacionais

This provides us with 946 citations to the original book and 169 to its Spanish translation. Unfortunately, Google Scholar has the tendency to ascribe all citations to a book to the latest edition of that book. Hence we cannot distinguish citations to the 1996 edition from citations to the 2006 edition.

Citations to individual chapters add 4000+ citations

More importantly, the screenshot below shows that another 4000+ citations can be found for citations to individual chapters within the handbook. Hence, only about a fifth of the total number of citations to the Handbook was to the handbook as a whole.

Journal impact analysis - Perform a citation analysis for one or more journals

Journal title: "Handbook of Organization Studies"
Exclude these words:
Year of publication between: and:
Data source: Google Scholar

Results

Papers:	26	Cites/paper:	154.00	h-index:	18	"Handbook of Organization Studies": all
Citations:	4004	Cites/author:	2378.00	g-index:	26	Query date: 2015-12-13
Years:	19	Papers/author:	15.57	hI,norm:	16	Papers: 26
Cites/year:	210.74	Authors/paper:	2.27	hI,annual:	0.84	Citations: 4004
						Years: 19

Cites	Per year	Authors	Title	Year	Publication
☑ h 898	99.78	M Alvesson, S Deetz	1.7 critical theory and postmodernism approaches to orga...	2006	...Sage handbook of organiz...
☑ h 748	83.11	MB Calás, L Smircich	1.8 From the 'Woman's Point of View'Ten Years Later: To...	2006	...Sage handbook of organiz...
☑ h 637	70.78	J Barney, W Hesterly	1.3 Organizational Economics: Understanding the Relation...	2006	...SAGE handbook of organi...
☑ h 358	39.78	M Reed	1.1 Organizational Theorizing: a Historically Contested Ter...	2006	The Sage handbook of orga...
☑ h 167	8.79	J Hassard	Images of time in work and organization	1996	Handbook of organization st...
☑ h 146	16.22	R Stablein	1.9 Data in Organization Studies	2006	The SAGE Handbook of Orga...
☑ h 145	16.11	K PARRY, A Bryman	I: 2.1 Leadership in Organizations	2006	...SAGE handbook of organi...
☑ h 129	14.33	B Flyvbjerg	Making organization research matter; power, values, and ...	2006	The Sage Handbook of Orga...
☑ h 112	12.44	S Maguire, B McKelvey, L Mira...	1.5 Complexity Science and Organization Studies	2006	...of organization studies
☑ h 97	10.78	TB Lawrence, R Suddaby	1.6 Institutions and Institutional Work	2006	...Handbook of Organization...
☑ h 94	10.44	R Greenwood, CR Hinings	Radical organizational change	2006	The Sage handbook of orga...

Smart searching allows a comprehensive case for impact

Needless to say, the editors of the Handbook above could make a much stronger case for the impact of the Handbook if they conducted a comprehensive citation search as described above. As edited volumes are an important way to publish state-of-the art research in some disciplines, it is very important to be able to conduct a comprehensive citation search for all references to the edited volume.

PoP tip 19: General citation search (1): Basic Search

The Publish or Perish **General citation search** page allows you to perform an Advanced Scholar Search query and analyse its results. This page contains a query pane with all parameters accepted by Google Scholar.

General citation search - Perform a general citation search			
Author(s):			
Publication:			
All of the words:			
Any of the words:			
None of the words:			
The phrase:			
Year of publication between:	0 and: 0		☐ Title words only
Data source:	Google Scholar ▼		

When to use the General citation search?

In many cases you will find that the **Author Impact** Search or the **Journal Impact** Search provides you with all the information you need.

However, there are some situations in which a **General citation search** might be helpful. The General citation search can be used for instance to:

- Find particular articles
- Find particular academics
- Conduct advanced author queries
- Conduct advanced journal queries
- Conduct an institutional search
- Conduct a literature review

Fields in the General citation search pane

The **Generical citation search** pane contains the following fields

Author(s)

Enter the names of the authors you want to look up. The recommended format is to use one or more initials and to quote each name, for example "A Harzing". Try to use the initials that the author usually publishes under. You can enter more than one name; this behaves as an AND clause (only co-authored paper), for example "A Harzing" "NG Noorderhaven". To perform an OR query (individual papers AND co-authored ones), include OR in the query: "A Harzing" OR "NG Noorderhaven"

Publication

Enter the name of the publication you want to look up. The recommended format is the full title enclosed in quotes, for example "*Journal of International Business*". However, you might have to experiment with common abbreviations as well.

Journal ISSN

If you are searching for a particular journal adding the ISSN will often get you a more accurate result.

All of the words

Enter any words that must all appear in the returned papers. This can be used to narrow down the search for a specific set of papers. If you use quotes around the words, this provides you with the same results as using **The phrase** field. If you include the search terms without quotes, it will provide many more matches as it matches the words in any order. Therefore, if the words are very generic there will be lots of publications that include them.

Any of the words

Enter any words that must appear alone or in combination in the returned papers. This can be used to narrow down the search for a specific set of papers. Unless the terms are very specific, it is usually not very effective to use this field without completing any of the other fields as you might get a lot of irrelevant results.

None of the words

Enter any words that must not appear in the returned papers. This can be used to narrow down the search for a specific set of papers.

The phrase

Enter a phrase (i.e., a specific sequence of words) that must all appear in the returned papers. This can be used to narrow down the search for a specific set of papers.

Year of publication between ... and ...

Enter the range of years in which the papers must have been published.

Title words only

Check this box to restrict the additional word matches (i.e., **All of the words**, **Any of the words**, **None of the words**, **The phrase**) to the titles of the returned papers; clear the box to match them anywhere in the papers.

PoP tip 20: General citation search (2): Finding a specific paper

The Publish or Perish General citation search can be used to find specific articles.

A familiar scenario: tracking down an article?

Does this scenario sound familiar? In a conversation at a conference or workshop, someone mentioned a recent journal article that you should really read, but you forgot both the author and the journal the paper was published in.

Smart searching through PoP finds your article in seconds

All you remember is some words in the title: Google Scholar and h-index. Of course you could search for the article in Google, but this is likely to provide you with many false hits. Using Google Scholar through Publish or Perish can – within seconds – provide you with a list of likely candidates. The screenshot shows the search in question.

General citation search - Perform a general citation search					
Author(s):					
Publication:					
All of the words:	"Google Scholar" h-index				
Any of the words:					
None of the words:					
The phrase:					
Year of publication between:	0	and:	0	☑ Title words only	
Data source:	Google Scholar ▼				

Results

Papers:	24	Cites/paper:	42.71	h-index:	12	"Google Scholar" h-index: all
Citations:	1025	Cites/author:	843.50	g-index:	24	Query date: 2015-12-13
Years:	7	Papers/author:	15.33	hI,norm:	9	Papers: 24
Cites/year:	146.43	Authors/paper:	2.00	hI,annual:	1.29	Citations: 1025
						Years: 7

Cites		Per year	Authors	Title	Year	Publication	Publisher
☑ h	429	61.29	J Bar-Ilan	Which h-index?—A comparison of WoS, Scopus and Go...	2008	Scientometrics	Springer
☑ h	183	30.50	AW Harzing, R Van Der Wal	A Google Scholar h-index for journals: An alternative m...	2009	Journal of the Ame...	Wiley Online Library
☑ h	96	13.71	P Jacsó	Testing the calculation of a realistic h-index in Google S...	2008	Library trends	muse.jhu.edu
☑ h	83	11.86	P Jacsó	The pros and cons of computing the h-index using Goo...	2008	Online information r...	emeraldinsight.com
☑ h	40	5.71	AW Harzing, R van der Wal	A Google Scholar H-Index for journals: A better metric ...	2008	Proceedings of the ...	researchgate.net
☑ h	39	13.00	SL De Groote, R Raszewski	Coverage of Google Scholar, Scopus, and Web of Scien...	2012	Nursing outlook	Elsevier
☑ h	29	4.83	P Jacsó	Calculating the h-index and other bibliometric and scien...	2009	Online Information ...	emeraldinsight.com
☑ h	27	6.75	DR Hodge, JR Lacasse	Ranking disciplinary journals with the Google Scholar h-i...	2011	Journal of Social W...	Taylor & Francis
☑ h	16	4.00	A Thor, L Bornmann	The calculation of the single publication h index and rel...	2011	Online Information ...	emeraldinsight.com
☑ h	15	5.00	P Jacsó	Using Google Scholar for journal impact factors and the...	2012	Online information r...	emeraldinsight.com
☑ h	14	2.00	AW Harzing, R van der Wal	Comparing the Google Scholar h-index with the ISI jour...	2008	Unpublished paper	harzing.com
☑ h	13	6.50	R Repiso, ED Lopez-Cozar	H Index Communication Journals according to Google S...	2013	arXiv preprint arXiv...	arxiv.org
☑	12	6.00	B Minasny, AE Hartemink, ...	Citations and the h index of soil researchers and journa...	2013	PeerJ	peerj.com

Result: your specific articles plus related papers

As we can immediately see there are only a couple of publications in the list, all recent. Although it was the most-cited article by Bar-Ilan you were interested in, you now also have a list of related articles that might of interest to you. Sorting these results per year also shows that several academics are posting recent papers on the arXiv preprint server, an excellent to keep readers informed of recent developments.

Cites		Per year	Authors	Title	Year	Publication	Publisher
☑	0	0.00	R van Bevern, C Komusiewi...	On Google Scholar H-Index Manipulation by Merging Articles	2014	arXiv preprint arXiv...	arxiv.org
☑	0	0.00	SJ Bensman, A Daugherty,...	Power-law distributions, the h-index, and Google Scholar (GS) citatio...	2014	arXiv preprint arXiv...	arxiv.org
☑	0	0.00	A Martin-Martin, E Ordunn...	Proceedings Scholar Metrics: H Index of proceedings on Computer Sc...	2014	arXiv preprint arXiv...	arxiv.org
☑ h	13	6.50	R Repiso, ED Lopez-Cozar	H Index Communication Journals according to Google Scholar Metrics ...	2013	arXiv preprint arXiv...	arxiv.org

PoP tip 21: General citation search (3): Finding a specific academic

The Publish or Perish General citation search can be used to find specific academics.

A familiar scenario: tracking down an academic?

Does this scenario sound familiar? You have attended your field's major academic conference and had a good conversation with someone you really want to follow up with. However, you did not get their business card and forgot their name.

Smart searching through PoP finds the academic in seconds

The only things you remember is that they were working at the University of Melbourne and published in the *Academy of Management of Learning & Education*, which is the journal you were talking about. You could go to the University of Melbourne website and review their staff list, but that might be a tedious process. You could go through the table of content of the *Academy of Management Learning & Education* hoping you remember their name.

However, what would be much simpler is to conduct the search below. This would allow you to refresh your memory in seconds and realize that you had been talking to me ☺ This search strategy will not always lead to such a quick result, but it is worth a try.

Google Scholar limitations: affiliation match not always perfect

Please note that this search is not flawless. Google Scholar does not have an "affiliation" field, hence the name of the university will be matched anywhere in the document. The results of our search contain ten articles. Of these only three match our intended search: two by myself, and one by a (former) colleague Ray Zammuto. All the other articles refer to the University of Melbourne somewhere in their paper.

PoP tip 22: General citation search (4): Advanced Author Queries

The Publish or Perish General citation search can be used for advanced author queries.

Finding out what specific authors have published on a specific topic

In the search on the Google Scholar h-index [General search: find articles], you noticed that there were two author names (Harzing and Jacsó) that occurred several times. You therefore wonder whether these authors have published additional work on Google Scholar.

To find out you can run an advanced author query by combining an author name with the words Google Scholar in the **All of the words** or **The phrase** field and ticking the title-words only box (see screenshot).

General citation search - Perform a general citation search

Author(s):	"P Jacso" OR "A Harzing"					
Publication:						
All of the words:	"Google Scholar"					
Any of the words:						
None of the words:						
The phrase:						
Year of publication between:	0	and: 0	☑ Title words only			
Data source:	Google Scholar					

Results

Papers:	54	Cites/paper:	39.74	h-index:	17	"P Jacso" OR "A Harzing", "Google Scholar": all
Citations:	2146	Cites/author:	1841.00	g-index:	46	Query date: 2015-12-13
Years:	11	Papers/author:	51.00	hI,norm:	17	Papers: 54 / Citations: 2146
Cites/year:	195.09	Authors/paper:	1.11	hI,annual:	1.55	Years: 11

Cites	Per year	Authors	Title	Year	Publication
☑ h 372	37.20	P Jacso	As we may search-Comparison of major features of the Web of Scien...	2005	CURRENT SCIENCE...
☑ h 371	46.38	AW Harzing, R Van der Wal	Google Scholar: the democratization of citation analysis	2007	Ethics in science an...
☑ h 297	29.70	P Jacsó	Google Scholar: the pros and the cons	2005	Online information r..
☑ h 183	30.50	AW Harzing, R Van Der Wal	A Google Scholar h-index for journals: An alternative metric to meas...	2009	Journal of the Ame...
☑ h 161	23.00	P Jacsó	Google scholar revisited	2008	Online information r..
☑ h 96	13.71	P Jacso	Testing the calculation of a realistic h-index in Google Scholar, Scopu...	2008	Library trends
☑ h 83	11.86	P Jacsó	The pros and cons of computing the h-index using Google Scholar	2008	Online information r..
☑ h 76	15.20	P Jacsó	Metadata mega mess in Google Scholar	2010	Online Information ...
☑ h 74	10.57	AW Harzing	Google Scholar-a new data source for citation analysis	2008	University of Melbo...
☑ h 65	32.50	AW Harzing	A preliminary test of Google Scholar as a source for citation data: a l...	2013	Scientometrics
☑ h 40	5.71	AW Harzing, R van der Wal	A Google Scholar H-Index for journals: A better metric to measure jo...	2008	Proceedings of the ...
☑ h 29	4.83	P Jacsó	Calculating the h-index and other bibliometric and scientometric indic...	2009	Online Information ...
☑ h 26	2.36	P Jacso	Google Scholar Beta	2004	Peter's Digital Refe...
☑ h 26	6.50	P Jacsó	Google Scholar duped and deduped-the aura of "robometrics"	2011	Online Information ...
☑ h 24	24.00	AW Harzing	A longitudinal study of Google Scholar coverage between 2012 and 2...	2014	Scientometrics
☑ h 20	2.00	P Jacso	Comparison and analysis of the citedness scores in Web of Science a...	2005	Digital libraries: Imp..
☑ h 18	3.60	P Jacsó	... and quality of research through rating and ranking of researchers ...	2010	Online information r..

Your notes

PoP tip 23: General citation search (5): What has a specific journal published on a topic?

The Publish or Perish General citation search is also very useful if you want to know what a particular journal or set of journals has published about a particular topic.

What has Science published on HIV before 1990?

For instance if you want to know what *Science* has published about HIV before 1990, an advanced journal query like the one below will give you the answer in less than a minute.

General citation search - Perform a general citation search

Author(s):	
Publication:	Science
All of the words:	HIV
Any of the words:	
None of the words:	
The phrase:	
Year of publication between:	and: 1989 ☑ Title words only
Data source:	Google Scholar ▾

Results

Papers:	55	Cites/paper:	425.89	h-index:	54	Science, HIV to 1989: all		
Citations:	23424	Cites/author:	6190.47	g-index:	55	Query date: 2015-12-13		
Years:	29	Papers/author:	14.92	hI,norm:	40	Papers: 55		
Cites/year:	807.72	Authors/paper:	4.31	hI,annual:	1.38	Citations: 23424 Years: 29		

Cites		Per year	Authors	Title	Year	Publication
☑ *h*	1681	64.65	BA Larder, G Darby, DD Ric...	HIV with reduced sensitivity to zid...	1989	Science
☑ *h*	1336	49.48	RW Price, B Brew, J Sidtis, ...	The brain in AIDS: central nervous...	1988	Science
☑ *h*	1260	48.46	BA Larder, SD Kemp	Multiple mutations in HIV-1 reverse...	1989	Science
☑ *h*	1127	38.86	CM Walker, DJ Moody, DP ...	CD8+ lymphocytes can control HIV...	1986	Science
☑ *h*	1101	40.78	CY Ou, S Kwok, SW Mitchell...	DNA amplification for direct detecti...	1988	Science
☑ *h*	1056	40.62	A Wlodawer, M Miller, M Ja...	Conserved folding in retroviral pro...	1989	Science
☑ *h*	965	35.74	BD Preston, BJ Poiesz, LA L...	Fidelity of HIV-1 reverse transcript...	1988	Science
☑ *h*	949	35.15	JD Roberts, K Bebenek, TA ...	The accuracy of reverse transcript...	1988	Science
☑ *h*	824	29.43	TM Folks, J Justement, A Ki...	Cytokine-induced expression of HI...	1987	Science
☑ *h*	803	29.74	C Cheng-Mayer, D Seto, M ...	Biologic features of HIV-1 that corr...	1988	Science
☑ *h*	767	29.50	SM Schnittman, MC Psallido...	The reservoir for HIV-1 in human p...	1989	Science
☑ *h*	612	22.67	JW Curran, HW Jaffe, AM ...	Epidemiology of HIV infection and ...	1988	Science
☑ *h*	567	20.25	DH Smith, RA Byrn, SA Mar...	Blocking of HIV-1 infectivity by a s...	1987	Science

What has JIBS published on emerging markets/economies?

Likewise, if you would like to know what the *Journal of International Business Studies* has published about emerging markets or emerging economies, you will find the most impactful publications in a few seconds.

General citation search - Perform a general citation search

Author(s):	
Publication:	Journal of International Business Studies
All of the words:	
Any of the words:	
None of the words:	
The phrase:	"emerging markets" OR "emerging economies"
Year of publication between:	0 and: 0 ☑ Title words only
Data source:	Google Scholar

Results

Papers:	27	Cites/paper:	155.33	h-index:	21	Journal of International Business Studies, "emerging markets" OR "emerging economies": all
Citations:	4194	Cites/author:	1836.47	g-index:	27	Query date: 2015-12-13
Years:	16	Papers/author:	11.23	hI,norm:	16	Papers: 27
Cites/year:	262.13	Authors/paper:	2.85	hI,annual:	1.00	Citations: 4194 Years: 16

Cites	Per year	Authors	Title	Year	Publication
☑ h 295	26.82	KE Meyer	Perspectives on multinational enterprises in emerging economies	2004	Journal of International Business Studies
☑ h 240	17.14	KE Meyer, S Estrin	Brownfield entry in emerging markets	2001	Journal of International Business Studies
☑ h 227	28.38	I Filatotchev, R Strange, J …	FDI by firms from newly industrialised economies in emerging mar…	2007	International Business …
☑ h 168	28.00	I Filatotchev, X Liu, T Buck…	The export orientation and export performance of high-technolo…	2009	of International Business …
☑ h 133	8.31	CJ Choi, SH Lee, JB Kim	A note on countertrade: contractual uncertainty and transaction …	1999	Journal of International Business Studies
☑ h 133	22.17	D Miller, J Lee, S Chang…	Filling the institutional void: The social behavior and performance …	2009	International Business …
☑ h 116	29.00	P Sharma	Country of origin effects in developed and emerging markets: Ex…	2011	Journal of International Business Studies
☑ h 114	12.67	KZ Zhou, KT David, JJ Li	Organizational changes in emerging economies: Drivers and cons…	2006	Journal of International Business …
☑ h 101	33.67	C Wang, J Hong, M Kafour…	Exploring the role of government involvement in outward FDI fro…	2012	of International Business …
☑ h 77	19.25	GD Bruton, S Khavul, H Cha…	Microlending in emerging economies: Building a new line of inquiry…	2011	of International Business …
☑ h 76	6.91	JP Doh, H Teegen, R Mudambi	Balancing private and state ownership in emerging markets' telec…	2004	of International Business …
☑ h 76	19.00	GD Santangelo, KE Meyer	Extending the internationalization process model: Increases and …	2011	International Business Studies
☑ h 64	12.80	X Liu, J Lu, I Filatotchev, T …	Returnee entrepreneurs, knowledge spillovers and innovation in …	2010	International Business …
☑ h 60	10.00	C Su, Z Yang, G Zhuang, N …	Interpersonal influence as an alternative channel communication …	2009	International Business …

PoP tip 24: General citation search (6): Institutional searches

The Publish or Perish General citation search can be used for very generic affiliation searches.

Google Scholar limitations: no bibliographic field for affiliation

Google Scholar does not have a bibliographic field for affiliation. This means that affiliation searches are not likely to be very accurate as Google Scholar will match the name of the university anywhere in the document (including acknowledgements, main body and references).

Generic searches might provide useful information

Without further experimentation and testing, I would therefore not recommend the use of Publish or Perish for these purposes. The only exception would be very generic searches, such as to establish whether a particular university generates any academic papers at all, which might be quite useful when evaluating potential international collaborations.

Combine affiliation with topic or journal

However, in spite of these limitations, Google Scholar does seem to have **some** use in finding out whether there are any academics in a particular institution working on a specific topic or publishing in a particular journal. This could be useful for instance for PhD students looking for a supervisor or for academics looking for an institution to visit on their sabbatical.

Example: JIBS articles published at the University of Melbourne

The screenshot below shows an example of such a search focusing on articles published in the *"Journal of International Business Studies"* at the University of Melbourne, my previous employer.

Cites		Per year	Rank	Authors	Title	Year
☑ h	392	30.15	1	J Evans, FT Mavondo	Psychic distance and organizational performance: An empirical exa...	2002
☑ h	30	1.58	2	AG Thompson	Compliance with agreements in cross-cultural transactions: some a...	1996
☑ h	76	9.50	3	S Johnston, B Menguc	Subsidiary size and the level of subsidiary autonomy in multinatin...	2007
☑ h	76	8.44	4	D Dow	Adaptation and performance in foreign markets: evidence of syste...	2006
☑ h	49	4.90	5	E Maitland, EL Rose...	How firms grow: clustering as a dynamic model of internationalization	2005
☑ h	404	44.89	6	D Dow, A Karunaratna	Developing a multidimensional instrument to measure psychic dista...	2006
☑ h	105	17.50	7	GRG Benito, B Petersen...	Towards more realistic conceptualisations of foreign operation modes	2009
☑ h	90	12.86	8	T Osegowitsch, A Sammartino	Reassessing (home-) regionalisation	2008
☑ h	88	14.67	9	BS Reiche, AW Harzing...	The role of international assignees' social capital in creating inter-u...	2009
☑	0	0.00	10	JM Cortina, T Köhler...	Restriction of variance interaction effects and their importance for...	2015
☑ h	196	32.67	11	N Noorderhaven, AW Harzing	Knowledge-sharing and social interaction within MNEs	2009
☑ h	34	17.00	12	H Tenzer, M Pudelko	The impact of language barriers on trust formation in multinational ...	2013
☑ h	42	10.50	13	BS Reiche, ML Kraimer...	Why do international assignees stay? An organizational em...	2011
☑	1	1.00	14	DW Baack, D Dow, R Parente...	Confirmation bias in individual-level perceptions of psychic distance...	2015
☑	6	6.00	15	S Volk, T Köhler, M Pudelko	Brain drain: The cognitive neuroscience of foreign language proces...	2014
☑ h	23	3.83	16	MS Jiang, PS Aulakh, Y Pan	Licensing duration in foreign markets: A real options perspective	2009
☑	1	1.00	17	E Maitland, A Sammartino	Managerial cognition and internationalization	2015
☑	0	0.00	18	MA Shaffer, BS Reiche, M Dimitro...	Work-and family-role adjustment of different types of global profe...	2015
☑	3	3.00	19	S Reiche, AW Harzing, M Pudelko	Why and how does shared language affect subsidiary knowledge i...	2015

In this type of search, it is generally best to sort the results by Google Scholar rank (by clicking on the rank column), rather than the standard sort for the number of citations. The latter privileges publications that have more citations, but these might be less relevant for the search in question.

Most results provide relevant information

Out of the 19 hits in the search, papers 1-15 and 17 were indeed written by one or more authors affiliated with Melbourne, whereas #18 and #19 both have the University of Melbourne mentioned as the PhD granting institution of Sebastian Reiche. The authors of publication #16 have no links to Melbourne, but refer to a working paper published at the University of Melbourne in their list of references.

Useful short-cut to identify relevant individuals at a university

This search might thus enable the student or academic to easily and very quickly identify relevant individuals in a particular university. However, it should be combined with other search strategies, such as perusing university web sites, for the best results.

PoP tip 25: Multi-query center (1): Introduction

The Publish or Perish **Multi-query center** page contains a list of recently executed queries. It also allows you to add further queries, optionally organized in folders that you want to keep for future reference.

Elements of the multi-query pane.

The multi-query pane consists of a toolbar across the top, a tree view on the left and a list view on the right, as shown in the following screen shot.

Query	Source	Papers	Cites	Cites/year	h	g	hI,norm	hI,annual	Query date
"A Harzing", "Journal of International ...	Google S...	0	0	0.00	0	0	0	0.00	13/12/2015
"Journal of International Business Stud...	Google S...	920	296423	6736.89	284	507	211	4.80	13/12/2015
"Handbook of Organization Studies": all	Google S...	26	4004	210.74	18	26	16	0.84	13/12/2015
hardy clegg nord: all	Google S...	36	1267	66.68	8	35	4	0.21	13/12/2015
"Journal of International Business Stud...	Google S...	188	1726	863.00	20	29	13	6.50	13/12/2015
"Journal of International Business Stud...	Google S...	140	10656	2131.20	57	95	39	7.80	13/12/2015
"Academy of Management Journal" fr...	Google S...	380	22199	4439.80	87	130	52	10.40	13/12/2015
Corporate diversification, executive co...	Google S...	1	5	2.50	1	1	1	0.50	13/12/2015
"Journal of Management", 0149-2063 f...	Google S...	0	0	0.00	0	0	0	0.00	13/12/2015
"a harzing": all	Google S...	298	9603	457.29	44	95	36	1.71	13/12/2015
"0021-9010" from 2014 to 2014: all	Google S...	200	945	315.00	13	19	7	2.33	13/12/2015

The results for individual queries are shown in a results pane that is identical the **Author Impact**, **Journal Impact** and **General citation** search pages.

Multi-query toolbar

Across the top of the multi-query pane is the toolbar that contains the commands for the Multi Query Center. Not all commands are available at all times; for some commands (for example, **Lookup** and **Lookup Direct**) you must first select a query in the list on the right before the command becomes active. Unavailable commands are grayed out.

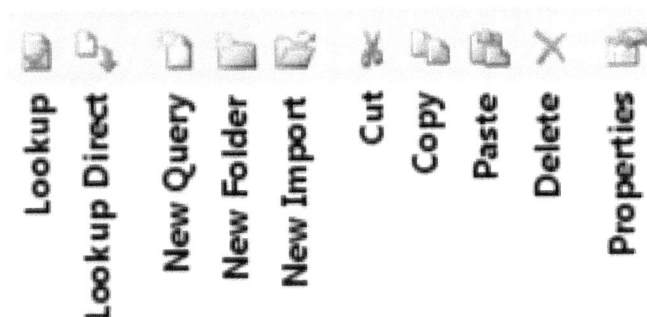

- **Lookup**: Looks up the current query, using the internal cache if possible. This means that if you have run the query before, the results will come from the cache and the search is not submitted to Google Scholar again. This is quicker and does not create unnecessary strain on Google Scholar.

- **Lookup Direct**: Looks up the current query, bypassing the internal cache and contacting Google Scholar directly. Only use Lookup Direct if you really want "fresh" data.
- **New Query**: Click this button to create a new query. It will be placed in the currently selected folder (or in the parent folder of the currently selected query).
- **New Folder**: Click this button to create a new query folder under the current folder. Please note that you can nest folders, i.e. you can make folders under the main **All Queries** folder, but you can also create as many levels of sub-folders as is useful to you.
- **Import Query**: Click this button to import external query data – such as ISI and Scopus data – into Publish or Perish. For more details see PoP tip 43.
- **Cut**: (shortcut Ctrl+X): Click this button to copy the currently selected folder or query to the Windows clipboard and delete it from its current position. You can then paste it into a different folder. Be careful if you are using this to move queries. For most users, it might be safer to use the mouse to drag the query or folder to a new folder.
- **Copy**: (shortcut Ctrl+C):Click this button to copy the currently selected folder or query to the Windows clipboard. You can then paste it into a different folder.
- **Paste**: (shortcut Ctrl+V): Click this button to paste the folder or query on the Windows clipboard into the current folder.
- **Delete**: (shortcut: use delete button): Click this button to delete the currently selected folder or query. If you delete a folder, all queries in it are also deleted. If you change your mind, you can retrieve the deleted folder from the Trash folder.
- **Properties**: (Shortcut Alt+Enter): Click this button to edit the currently selected folder or query.

PoP tip 26: Multi-query center (2): Tree view

The tree on the left of the Publish or Perish **Multi-query center** displays the available query folders. The folders are containers that help you organize your queries.

Query folder management

Query folders can be nested, and they can be rearranged by dragging and dropping with the mouse, just like you would do in Internet Explorer. They can also be copied **(Ctrl+C)**, cut **(Ctrl+X)**, and pasted **(Ctrl+V)**.

Recent queries folder

The tree always contains the **Recent Queries** folder. This folder automatically receives the queries that you perform on one of the other citation analysis pages. You can also add your own queries to this folder and edit existing queries. However, you cannot delete this folder or change its name.

Example of nested folders for effective query management

The screenshot below shows how queries can be nested to create logical containers for your queries. I strongly recommend you to organize your queries if you are planning to run them on a regular basis. It can be easy to get lost in a long list of recent queries.

Query	Papers	Cites	Cites/year
"Alessie R" from 1988: all	192	2431	93.50
"Anufriev M" from 2004: all	57	300	30.00
"Baillon A", NOT "AF Baillon" insecticida...	29	312	44.57
"Baltussen R" from 1996: all	170	3331	185.06
"Barkema Harry" OR "Barkema HG" fro...	54	6693	334.65
"Beck Thorsten", NOT "WO Patent" "US ...	426	24753	1650.20
"Beetsma R" from 1994: all	272	3538	176.90
"Belderbos R" from 1992: all	213	3594	163.36
"Benschop Y" from 1996: all	92	1435	79.72
"Beugelsdijk S" from 2001: all	121	2391	183.92
"Bijmolt T" from 1994: all	147	2059	102.95
"Blazevic V", NOT cancer norovirus epito...	54	372	33.82
"Bleichrodt H" from 1995: all	162	3845	202.37
"Bloemen Hans" OR "HG Bloemen", NO...	72	614	36.12
"Bloemer J", NOT "JW Bloemer" "JF Bloe...	176	4673	186.92
"Boone Jan", NOT "J* Boone" sports fro...	146	1900	135.71
"Boot A", NOT "AM Boot" "AJM Boot" "...	400	7478	276.96
"Borghans L" from 1996: all	292	2564	142.44
"Borm Peter" OR "Borm PEM", NOT "PJ...	290	2346	102.00
"Boswijk P" OR "Boswijk HP" from 1992: ...	129	1298	59.00

Tree folder list:
- All queries
  - Recent queries
  - Older queries
  - A-Archive
    - ABS conference
    - AoM presidents
    - DOMM benchmarking
    - Nobel prize winners
    - PoP Book queries
  - A-Harzing longitudinal
  - A-Old research projects
    - Economen top 40
    - GS - ISI - Scopus
    - Nobel prize winners
    - Open Access
  - ERC Advanced Grant
  - HROB
  - Institutions
  - Language review
  - PoP Blog
  - Satu project
  - Trash

Multi-query center - Manage and compare multiple citation queries

Clean out your recent query folder periodically

It is also a good idea to clean out your Recent Queries folder periodically, so that even if you do not want to make the effort to organize your queries into folders, you can keep some order in your queries. Simply select the query you want to discard and click on the delete button in the toolbar, or hit the delete button on your keyboard.

PoP tip 27: Multi-query center (3): List view

The list on the right of the Publish or Perish **Multi-query center** displays queries similar to the queries that you enter on the other pages, but presented in a condensed format.

Queries can be moved and copied

Queries can be moved between folders by dragging and dropping them with the mouse. They can also be copied **(Ctrl+C)**, cut **(Ctrl+X)**, and pasted **(Ctrl+V)**.

Example of results in multi-query center

The screenshot below shows the full results of the queries shown in the Multi-query centre tree view. Please note that the results can be sorted on any column: simply click on the column heading. By default the queries are sorted in the order in which they were executed. The list below has been sorted by hI,annual.

Query	Papers	Cites	Cites/year	h	g	hI,norm	hI,annual	Query date
G "Beck Thorsten", NOT "WO Patent" "US ...	426	24753	1650.20	60	155	43	2.87	20/01/2014
G "Tol Richard" OR "RSJ Tol" from 1993: all	808	17404	828.76	68	116	46	2.19	21/01/2014
G "Verhoef Peter" OR "PC Verhoef", NOT "...	163	6018	462.92	37	77	26	2.00	21/01/2014
G "Frenken K" from 1999: all	272	5493	366.20	36	72	29	1.93	21/01/2014
G "Kolk Ans" from 1996: all	157	5512	306.22	41	73	33	1.83	21/01/2014
G "Harzing A" from 1995: all	202	6372	335.37	40	78	32	1.68	27/01/2014
G "Demerouti E" from 1996: all	210	12408	689.33	44	111	29	1.61	21/01/2014
G "Raven Rob" OR "R.P.J.M. Raven" from 2...	91	1899	189.90	24	43	16	1.60	21/01/2014
G "van Knippenberg D" OR "D Knippenber...	258	9439	449.48	50	95	33	1.57	25/01/2014
G "Verspagen B" OR "HHG Verspagen" fro...	385	9836	393.44	52	94	39	1.56	21/01/2014
G "de Ruyter Ko" OR "JC de Ruyter" OR "K...	244	9900	471.43	47	98	32	1.52	25/01/2014
G "Volberda H" from 1992: all	328	11036	501.64	43	103	33	1.50	21/01/2014

List view columns

The list view displays the following columns. At present it is not possible to change the columns that are displayed, but this might change in a future version of Publish or Perish.

Column	Description
Query	An abbreviated rendering of the query parameters, intended as a reminder about the query. To see all query parameters, press **Alt+Enter** to open the Edit Query dialog box.
Source	The source of data (e.g. Google Scholar, ISI, Scopus, Microsoft Academic Search)
Papers	The number of results (~papers) returned by the query.
Cites	The total number of citations returned by the query.
Cites/year	The total number of citations in the query divided by the number of years spanned by the results.
h	Hirsch's h-index calculated for the query results.

g	Egge's g-index calculated for the query results.
hI,norm	Normalized individual h-index for the query results.
hI,annual	Annualized individual h-index for the query results.
Query Date	The date on which this query was last performed.
Cache Date	The date on which the query data were last retrieved from Google Scholar.

PoP tip 28: Multi-query center (4): Exporting

The Publish or Perish **Multi-query center** not only makes it easier to **organize** your queries, it also makes it easier to **export** the results for further processing. This is particularly useful if you want to do further bibliometric research with the PoP results.

Easy exporting through popup menu

The easiest way to export results is to select the queries you want to export and right-click to access the popup menu. Let's assume we are working with a set of Dutch Economists as I did for the project in this paper.

- Harzing, A.W.; Mijnhardt, W. (2015) **Proof over promise: Towards a more inclusive ranking of Dutch academics in Economics & Business**, *Scientometrics*, vol. 102, no. 1, pp. 727-749.

Query	Papers	Cites	Cites/year	h	g	hI,nor...	hI,annual	Query date
"Alessie R" from 1988: all	192	2431	93.50	23	46	15	0.58	20/01/2014
"Anufriev M" from 2004: all	57	300	30.00	10	16	7	0.70	20/01/2014
"Baillon A", NOT "AF Baillon" ins...	29	312	44.57	8	17	5	0.71	20/01/2014
"Baltussen R" from 1996: all	170	3331	185.06	31	54	18	1.00	20/01/2014
"Barkema Harry" OR "Barkema H...	54	6693	334.65	19	54	17	0.85	20/01/2014
"Beck Thorsten", NOT "WO Paten...	426	24753	1650.20	60	155	43	2.87	20/01/2014
"Beetsma R" from 1994: all	272	3538	176.90	31	57	23	1.15	20/01/2014
"Belderbos R" from 1992: all	213	3594	163.36	25	59	20	0.91	20/01/2014
"Benschop Y" from 1996: all	92	1435	79.72	19	37	14	0.78	20/01/2014
"Beugelsdijk S" from 2001: all	121	2391	183.92	27	48	19	1.46	20/01/2014

Tree items: All queries; Recent queries; Older queries; A-Archive; A-Old research projects; Economen top 40; 2003-2013; Alternative spellir; Update; GS - ISI - Scopus; Nobel prize winners; Open Access

Export the results

If you would like to export the **results**, i.e. the articles published by the Economists in question, you would select one of the **Save As ....** Commands, which allow you to save and import the data into for instance Endnote (Save As Endnote), or MS Excel (Save as CSV). Simply select any queries you want to export (as many as you want), right-click and select **Save as CSV** or **Save as Endnote**. For other export options, please refer to the PoP help file.

Export the statistics

If you would like to export the **statistics** for the Economists in question, i.e. their number of papers, citations, h-index etc., you would select one of the **Copy Statistics ....** commands, which allow you to copy the statistics to the Windows clipboard for pasting into a variety of other programs.

Copy statistics for Excel is a good default option

For most users the best option is to use the Copy Statistics for Excel command. In order to ensure you copy the headers with the names of the statistics into your file, use **Copy Statistics for Excel with Header**. Then paste the results into an Excel worksheet. With one click you insert a table and your data are ready for further processing.

Query	Papers	Citations	Years	Cites_Year	Cites_Paper	Cites_Author	Papers_Author	Authors_Paper
Alessie R from 1988: all	192	2431	26	93.5	12.66	913.15	70.95	3.01
Anufriev M from 2004: all	57	300	10	30	5.26	146.5	26.1	2.51
Baillon A, NOT "AF Baillon" ins	29	312	7	44.57	10.76	113	12.62	2.79
Baltussen R from 1996: all	170	3331	18	185.06	19.59	993.28	50.25	3.79
Barkema Harry OR "Barkema I	54	6693	20	334.65	123.94	2924.03	23.69	2.72
Beck Thorsten, NOT "WO Pate	426	24753	15	1650.2	58.11	9735.52	206.32	2.67
Beetsma R from 1994: all	272	3538	20	176.9	13.01	1749.43	128.88	2.52
Belderbos R from 1992: all	213	3594	22	163.36	16.87	1724.77	95.7	2.84
Benschop Y from 1996: all	92	1435	18	79.72	15.6	761.29	43.87	2.63
Beugelsdijk S from 2001: all	121	2391	13	183.92	19.76	1258.61	59.72	2.53
Bijmolt T from 1994: all	147	2059	20	102.95	14.01	754.63	57.48	3.06
Blazevic V, NOT cancer norovi	54	372	11	33.82	6.89	153.16	29.12	2.59
Bleichrodt H from 1995: all	162	3845	19	202.37	23.73	1726.09	72.61	2.75
Bloemen Hans OR "HG Bloem	72	614	17	36.12	8.53	446.46	43.39	2.28

PoP tip 29: Multi-query center (5): Importing (1): Re-Importing exported Publish or Perish data

As described in the section on exporting, you can export the results of a query to for instance Excel. Subsequently you can re-import this file into Publish or Perish.

Making corrections to results and recalculate stats

This can be useful if you want to make minor corrections to the results and then have PoP recalculate the statistics. You might for instance want to:

- Adjust years that Google Scholar parsed wrongly.
- Complete truncated titles or author lists.
- Correct titles for records where Google Scholar parsed the wrong version of the paper as a master record.
- Remove irrelevant publications altogether, instead of un-ticking them in PoP. This will make it easier to subsequently clean up the results further by merging as you have fewer records to work with.

Procedure

In order to do follow these steps:

1. Right-click on the query you wish to export.
2. Chose **Save as CSV** and give the file a meaningful name.
3. Open the file in Excel by double-clicking on it. [**Note**: Don't worry if you see strange squiggly letters; this is just Excel not coping well with accented letters. They will be fine once you reimport the data into PoP].
4. Make the required changes.
5. Save the file again in CSV format. [**Note**: if you use a Mac, you will have to use **Save as *Windows* CSV**, Don't ask me why: long story, Mac format doesn't play nice].
6. Reimport the file into Publish or Perish by clicking on the **New Import** icon (see Multiquery Center).

Worked example: corrected data

As an example the two screenshots below show my six most highly cited publications (unmerged) on a citations per year basis. The first screenshot shows the original data. The second screenshot shows the corrected data. Changes made were:

- Change the year for the third publication from 2007 to 2008, the correct publication year.
- Change the year for a publication parsed as 2013 (as online first publication date) to 2014 (as print publication date). [See also Google Scholar: Inconsistent year].
- Change the title for the third publication into its correct title (the reported title is the title of an earlier working paper).

Old results

Cites		Per year	Authors	Title	Year
☑	**h** 436	72.67	NJ Adler, AW H...	When knowledge wins: Transcending the sense and nonsense of academic rankings	2009
☑	**h** 342	68.40	AW Harzing, A ...	International human resource management	2010
☑	**h** 372	46.50	AW Harzing, R ...	Google Scholar: the democratization of citation analysis	2007
☑	**h** 305	55.88	AW Harzing	Publish or perish	2007
☑	**h** 450	36.31	AW Harzing	Acquisitions versus greenfield investments: International strategy and management of entry modes	2002
☑	**h** 164	32.80	AW Harzing	The publish or perish book	2010

New results

Cites		Per year	Authors	Title	Year
☑	**h** 436	72.67	NJ Adler, AW Harzing	When knowledge wins: Transcending the sense and nonsense of academic rankings	2009
☑	**h** 342	68.40	AW Harzing, A Pinnin...	International human resource management	2010
☑	**h** 372	53.14	AW Harzing, R Van d...	Google Scholar: a new source for citation analysis	2008
☑	**h** 305	38.13	AW Harzing	Publish or perish	2007
☑	**h** 450	34.62	AW Harzing	Acquisitions versus greenfield investments: International strategy and management of entry modes	2002
☑	34	34.00	H Tenzer, M Pudelko	The impact of language barriers on trust formation in multinational teams	2014

Effect of the corrections

As a result, the citations per year for the third paper increased from 46.50 per year to 53.14 per year. Changes for the language barrier and trust formation paper were more dramatic as its citations per year increased from 17 to 34, making it my 6th most highly cited paper per year instead of my 27th most highly cited.

Conclusion

Obviously, one would not go through the effort of manually correcting the results for every single search. However, the ability to make corrections and re-import the data might be a life-saver for one-off important occasions such as an application for tenure or promotion.

PoP tip 30: Multi-query center (6): Importing (2): Importing ISI data

If your university has a subscription to the Web of Science, you can also import data from this database into Publish or Perish, allowing you to calculate a large variety of metrics with data from this database.

Importing saved ISI searches

Unfortunately direct access of this data-source is not technically possible through Publish or Publish even if your university subscribes to it. However, you can run and save searches in the Web of Science and import those into Google Scholar.

ISI import in five easy steps

1. Conduct a search in the Web of Science. [If you don't know how to do this, contact your librarian].
2. Once you have the correct set of results, click on the drop-down field **Save to Other File For...** (see screenshot). Click on **Save to Other File Formats**.

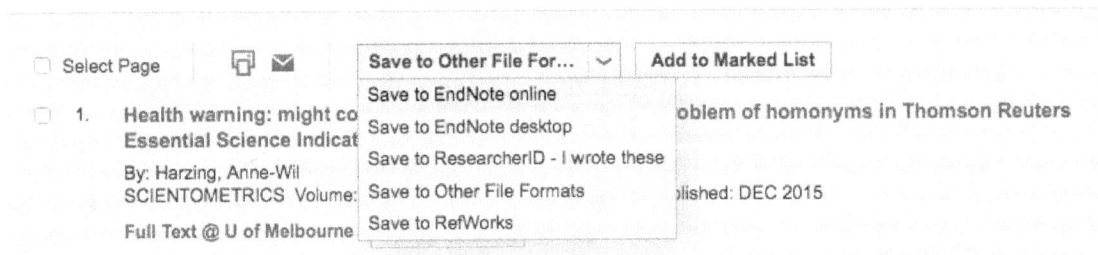

3. On the resulting pop-up box (see screenshot), you can leave all the settings to default, unless you have more than one page of results. In that case, specify the number of records you want to export.

4. This provides you with a .txt file that you can import into Publish or Perish, simply by clicking on the New Import icon [see multi-query center] or by clicking **File/Import External Data**.

5. You will then see the following screenshot. Click on OK and Publish or Perish will import the ISI data into the multi-query center. The results will appear in the folder that you are in when you import the data.

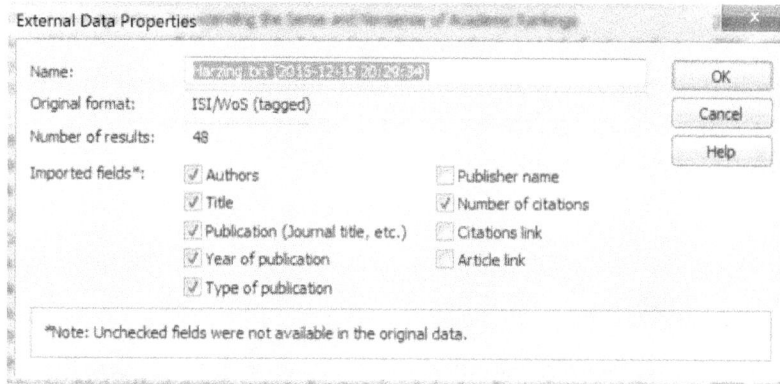

The result: a compact list of publications ready for further analysis

The result is a neat list of publications that can then be sorted in any way you want. Statistics and results can be exported for further analyses just like the results of Google Scholar searches.

Results

Papers:	47	Cites/paper:	35.87	h-index:	20	Harzing Web of Science.txt [2015-12-15 20:29:34]
Citations:	1686	Cites/author:	1111.75	g-index:	41	Query date: 2015-12-15
Years:	15	Papers/author:	26.16	hI,norm:	16	Papers: 47
Cites/year:	112.40	Authors/paper:	3.00	hI,annual:	1.07	Citations: 1686
						Years: 15

Cites	Per year	Authors	Title	Year	Publication
☑ h 203	33.83	Nancy J. Adler, Anne-Wil Harzing	When Knowledge Wins: Transcending the...	2009	ACADEMY OF MANAGEMENT LEARNING & EDUCATION
☑ h 138	10.62	AW Harzing	Acquisitions versus greenfield investment...	2002	STRATEGIC MANAGEMENT JOURNAL
☑ h 129	9.21	AW Harzing	Of bears, bumble-bees, and spiders: The ...	2001	JOURNAL OF WORLD BUSINESS
☑ h 112	9.33	AW Harzing, A Sorge	The relative impact of country of origin an...	2003	ORGANIZATION STUDIES
☑ h 99	6.60	AW Harzing	An empirical analysis and extension of the...	2000	JOURNAL OF INTERNATIONAL BUSINESS STUDIES
☑ h 88	6.29	AW Harzing	Who's in charge? An empirical study of ex...	2001	HUMAN RESOURCE MANAGEMENT
☑ h 87	14.50	Niels Noorderhaven, Anne-Wil Harzing	Knowledge-sharing and social interaction ...	2009	JOURNAL OF INTERNATIONAL BUSINESS STUDIES
☑ h 80	13.33	Anne-Wil Harzing, Ron van der Wal	A Google Scholar h-Index for Journals: A...	2009	JOURNAL OF THE AMERICAN SOCIETY FOR INFORM/
☑ h 80	5.33	AW Harzing	Cross-national industrial mail surveys - W...	2000	INDUSTRIAL MARKETING MANAGEMENT
☑ h 78	9.75	Markus Pudelko, Anne-Wil Harzing	Country-of-origin, localization, or domina...	2007	HUMAN RESOURCE MANAGEMENT
☑ h 59	5.36	JB Hocking, M Brown, AW Harzing	A knowledge transfer perspective of strat...	2004	INTERNATIONAL JOURNAL OF HUMAN RESOURCE M/
☑ h 56	4.31	AW Harzing	Are our referencing errors undermining o...	2002	JOURNAL OF ORGANIZATIONAL BEHAVIOR
☑ h 46	5.75	John Mingers, Anne-Wil Harzing	Ranking journals in business and manage...	2007	EUROPEAN JOURNAL OF INFORMATION SYSTEMS
☑ h 44	7.33	B. Sebastian Reiche, Anne-Wil Harz...	The role of international assignees' social ...	2009	JOURNAL OF INTERNATIONAL BUSINESS STUDIES
☑ h 36	4.00	AW Harzing, N Noorderhaven	Knowledge flows in MNCs: An empirical te...	2006	INTERNATIONAL BUSINESS REVIEW
☑ h 34	4.25	J. Barry Hocking, Michelle Brown, A...	Balancing global and local strategic conte...	2007	HUMAN RESOURCE MANAGEMENT
☑ h 31	7.75	Anne-Wil Harzing, Kathrin Koester, ...	Babel in business: The language barrier a...	2011	JOURNAL OF WORLD BUSINESS
☑ h 29	2.64	B Myloni, AWK Harzing, H Mirza	Host country specific factors and the tran...	2004	INTERNATIONAL JOURNAL OF MANPOWER
☑ h 28	14.00	Anne-Wil Harzing	A preliminary test of Google Scholar as a ...	2013	SCIENTOMETRICS
☑ h 21	10.50	Anne-Wil Harzing	Document categories in the ISI Web of Kn...	2013	SCIENTOMETRICS
☑ 19	9.50	Anne-Wil Harzing, Markus Pudelko	Language competencies, policies and prac...	2013	JOURNAL OF WORLD BUSINESS

PoP tip 31: Multi-query center (7): Importing (3): Importing Scopus data

If your university has a subscription to Scopus, you can also import data from this database into Publish or Perish, allowing you to calculate a large variety of metrics with data from this database.

Importing saved Scopus searches

Unfortunately direct access of this data-source is not technically possible through Publish or Publish even if your university subscribes to it. However, you can run and save searches in Scopus and import those into Google Scholar.

Scopus import in five easy steps

1. Conduct a search in Scopus. [If you don't know how to do this, contact your librarian].
2. Once you have the correct set of results, click on the drop-down field next to the check-box and click **Select all** to select all 62 records.

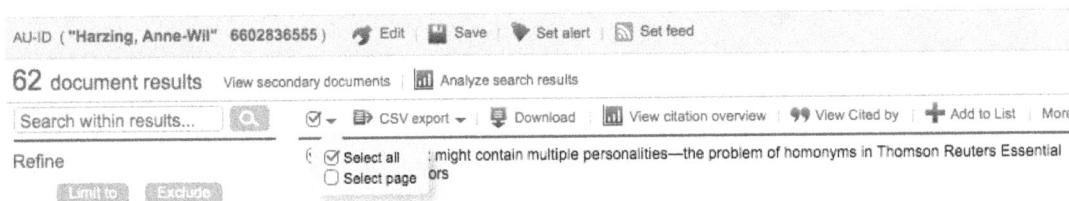

3. Click on the drop-down field next to export. You will get a pop-up menu. On that menu, select CSV export and save the file with a meaningful name. Do **not** change anything under "Choose the information to be exported". Doing so will make the file unreadable for Publish or Perish.

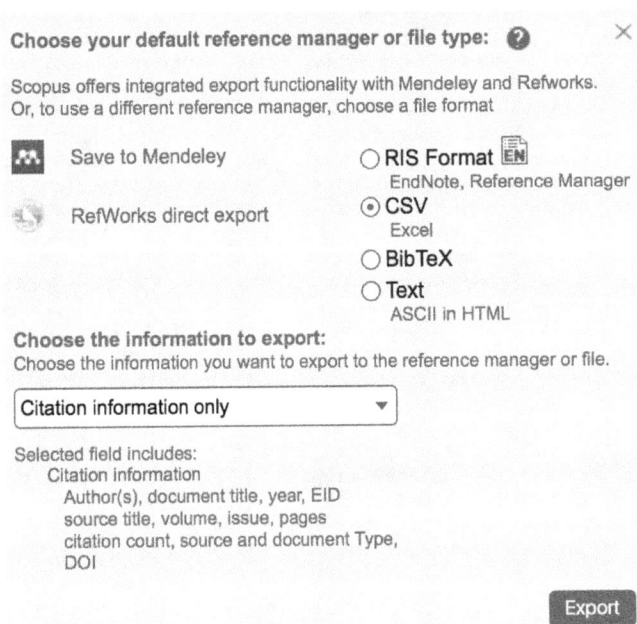

4. This provides you with a .csv file that you can import into Publish or Perish, simply by clicking on the New Import icon [See multi-query center] or by clicking **File/Import External Data**.

5. You will then see the following screenshot. Click on OK and Publish or Perish will import the Scopus data into the multi-query center. The results will appear in the folder that you are in when you import the data.

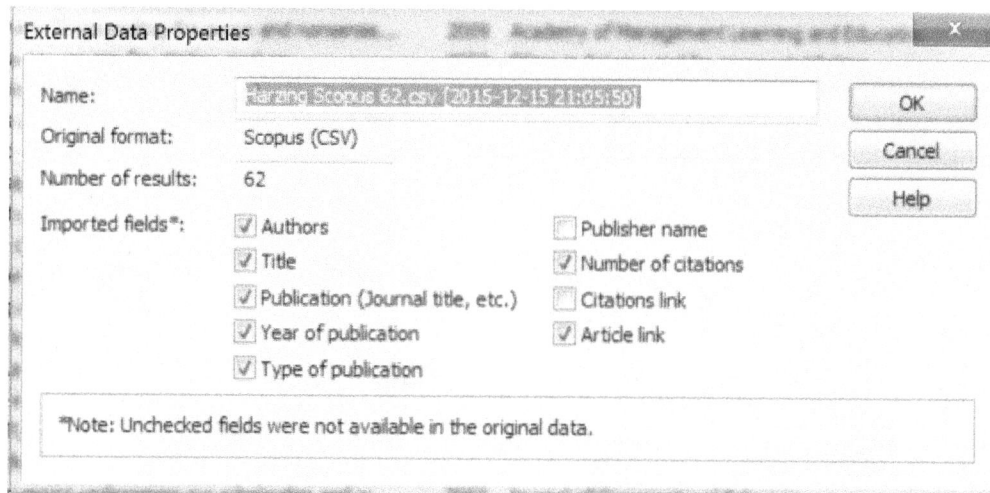

The result: a compact list of publications ready for further analysis

The result is a neat list of publications that can then be sorted in any way you want. Statistics and results can be exported for further analyses just like the results of Google Scholar searches.

Results

Papers:	62	Cites/paper:	42.82	h-index:	25	Harzing Scopus 62.csv [2015-12-15 21:05:50]
Citations:	2655	Cites/author:	1874.05	g-index:	51	Query date: 2015-12-15
Years:	18	Papers/author:	34.38	hI,norm:	20	Papers: 62
Cites/year:	147.50	Authors/paper:	3.13	hI,annual:	1.11	Citations: 2655
						Years: 18

Cites		Per year	Authors	Title	Year	Publication
✓	h 216	36.00	N.J. Adler, A.-W. Harzing	When knowledge wins: Transcending the sense and nonsense...	2009	Academy of Management Learning and Education
✓	h 176	25.14	A.-W.K. Harzing, R. van...	Google Scholar as a new source for citation analysis	2008	Ethics in Science and Environmental Politics
✓	h 174	9.67	A.-W. Harzing	Response rates in international mail surveys: Results of a 22-...	1997	International Business Review
✓	h 173	13.31	A.-W. Harzing	Acquisitions versus greenfield investments: International stra...	2002	Strategic Management Journal
✓	h 154	11.00	A.-W. Harzing	Of bears, bumble-bees, and spiders: The role of expatriates i...	2001	Journal of World Business
✓	h 148	9.87	A.-W. Harzing	An empirical analysis and extension of the Bartlett and Ghosh...	2000	Journal of International Business Studies
✓	h 144	12.00	A.-W. Harzing, A. Sorge	The relative impact of country of origin and universal continge...	2003	Organization Studies
✓	h 135	15.00	A.-W. Harzing	Response styles in cross-national survey research: A 26-coun...	2006	International Journal of Cross Cultural Management
✓	h 99	7.07	A.-W. Harzing	Who's in charge? An empirical study of executive staffing pra...	2001	Human Resource Management
✓	h 95	15.83	N. Noorderhaven, A.-W...	Knowledge-sharing and social interaction within MNEs	2009	Journal of International Business Studies
✓	h 93	11.63	M. Pudelko, A.-W. Harzing	Country-of-origin, localization, or dominance effect? An empiri...	2007	Human Resource Management
✓	h 93	6.20	A.-W. Harzing	Cross-national industrial mail surveys: Why do response rates...	2000	Industrial Marketing Management
✓	h 83	13.83	A-W. Harzing, R.V.D. Wal	A google scholar h-index for journals: An alternative metric to...	2009	Journal of the American Society for Information Science...
✓	h 76	6.33	A.-W. Harzing	THE ROLE OF CULTURE IN ENTRY-MODE STUDIES: FROM NE...	2003	Advances in International Management
✓	h 68	6.18	J.B. Hocking, M. Brown,...	A knowledge transfer perspective of strategic assignment pur...	2004	International Journal of Human Resource Management
✓	h 62	5.17	A.-W. Harzing	Are our referencing errors undermining our scholarship and cr...	2003	Journal of Organizational Behavior
✓	h 55	6.88	J. Mingers, A.-W. Harzing	Ranking journals in business and management: A statistical an...	2007	European Journal of Information Systems
✓	h 55	5.50	A.-W. Harzing	Does the use of English-language questionnaires in cross-nati...	2005	International Journal of Cross Cultural Management
✓	h 48	8.00	B.S. Reiche, A.-W. Harz...	The role of international assignees' social capital in creating in...	2009	Journal of International Business Studies
✓	h 48	5.33	A.-W. Harzing, N. Noor...	Knowledge flows in MNCs: An empirical test and extension of ...	2006	International Business Review
✓	h 42	5.25	J.B. Hocking, M. Brown,...	Balancing global and local strategic contexts: Expatriate know...	2007	Human Resource Management
✓	h 37	3.36	B. Myloni, A.-W.K. Harz...	Host country specific factors and the transfer of human resou...	2004	International Journal of Manpower
✓	h 35	8.75	A.-W. Harzing, K. Köste...	Babel in business: The language barrier and its solutions in th...	2011	Journal of World Business
✓	h 33	16.50	A.-W. Harzing	A preliminary test of Google Scholar as a source for citation d...	2013	Scientometrics
✓	h 25	2.27	B. Myloni, A.-W. Harzin...	Human Resource Management in Greece: Have the colours of...	2004	International Journal of Cross Cultural Management
✓	23	3.83	A.-W. Harzing, J. Baldu...	Rating versus ranking: What is the best way to reduce respo...	2009	International Business Review
✓	20	10.00	A.-W. Harzing, M. Pudelko	Language competencies, policies and practices in multinational...	2013	Journal of World Business

Comparing metrics across data-sources

Even if you are not doing any bibliometric research, the multi-query center allows you to instantly compare citation metrics from different data-sources. The screenshot below shows that in my case there is quite a big difference between the three data-sources. As discussed in From h-index to hIa: The ins and outs of research metrics, this is quite typical for a Social Science scholar.

Query	Source	Papers	Cites	Cites/year	h	g	hI,norm	hI,annual
Harzing Google Scholar: all	Google Scholar	297	9614	480.70	44	95	36	1.80
Harzing Scopus.csv [2015-1...	Scopus (CSV)	62	2655	147.50	25	51	20	1.11
Harzing Web of Science.txt ...	ISI/WoS (tagged)	47	1686	112.40	20	41	16	1.07

Your notes

PoP tip 32: Multi-query center (8): Exporting and Importing Archives

Having spent a lot of time on creating queries and logical folder structures in the multi-query center, you obviously do not want to go through this entire process a second or even third time. This might be necessary in the following situations:

- Transferring your work after buying a new computer.
- Reinstating your work after a computer hard-disk crash.
- Sharing your queries with a research collaborator or research assistant.

Whatever the reason, Publish or Perish has a sophisticated system for archiving your data, and exporting or importing them.

Archiving your data

To save your Publish or Perish queries and the associated results data to an archive, use the **Export to Archive** command. You can subsequently reload these data into Publish or Perish on the same computer or on a different computer through the **Import from Archive** command.

Publish or Perish data archives store the following information:

- The selected queries and their parameters,
- The query results,
- The metrics for the query results,
- The folder structure that contains the queries that are being exported.

Exporting the data archive

To export the Publish or Perish data archive, use the following procedure.

1. Go to the multi-query center.
2. Select the queries or the folder to export, or the **All queries** root to export the entire queries tree.
3. Right-click on the selected item and choose **Export to Archive**, or choose **File > Export to Archive** from the main menu.
4. When prompted, enter a file name for the data archive and click **Save**.

Publish or Perish will then save the queries with all their parameters and their metrics, plus the complete results for each query. The resulting archive file has a .pxa file extension and can be used to import the same queries and their data into Publish or Perish on the same or a different computer.

Importing the data archive

To import a Publish or Perish data archive that you or someone else previously exported, use the following procedure.

1. Choose **File > Import from Archive** from the main menu.
2. When prompted, select the archive that you want to import and click **Open**.

Publish or Perish will then load the queries and their data from the archive and merge them into your existing queries tree in the multi-query center. Unless the file is very large, this typically takes only a few seconds, so if you think nothing happened you probably just blinked ☺.

Rules applied when merging queries

While merging, Publish or Perish applies the following rules:

- If an incoming query is the same as an existing query, the existing query is overwritten if the incoming data are newer. If the incoming data are older than the existing data, no change is made.
- If an incoming query has no counterpart in the existing tree, it is simply added to the tree.
- If an incoming folder is already present in the existing tree, its contents are merged with the existing folder's contents.
- If an incoming folder is not yet present in the existing tree, it is added to the tree and its contents are then processed further.

The nitty gritty details....

During the merge process, Publish or Perish uses internal IDs to track individual queries and folders. The purpose of these IDs is to locate the correct queries and folders even if they have been moved to a new location in the existing tree after the data archive was originally exported. On occasion, this might cause imported queries or folders to show up in a different location than they were in when originally exported, but that is by design and avoids duplicating the information in the old and the new tree locations.

PoP tip 33: Multi-query center (9): Longitudinal comparisons

The Publish or Perish **Multi-query center** is also very useful if you want to run the same query periodically to compare metrics over time.

Copy queries before re-running them

In order to ensure you keep the results of older queries intact, you need to copy the query and run the copied query again. If you run the original query again, the old results will be replaced by the new data.

Worked example: longitudinal author search

I have a folder in which I keep monthly queries for my own name since May 2013. Longitudinal results for individuals might be important to establish progress for a tenure, promotion, or grant application.

Query	Papers	Cites	Cites/year	h	g	hI,norm	hI,annual	Query date
G "A Harzing"...	198	5344	296.89	36	70	32	1.78	02/05/2013
G "A Harzing"...	199	5459	303.28	37	71	32	1.78	02/06/2013
G "A Harzing"...	200	5714	317.44	38	73	32	1.78	01/07/2013
G "A Harzing"...	201	5730	318.33	37	73	32	1.78	12/08/2013
G "A Harzing"...	202	5815	323.06	37	74	32	1.78	01/09/2013
G "A Harzing"...	202	5927	329.28	37	74	32	1.78	04/10/2013
G "A Harzing"...	205	6041	335.61	37	75	32	1.78	02/11/2013
G "A Harzing"...	204	6154	341.89	39	76	32	1.78	01/12/2013
G "A Harzing"...	207	6322	332.74	39	77	32	1.68	03/01/2014
G "A Harzing"...	207	6451	339.53	40	78	33	1.74	31/01/2014
G "A Harzing"...	223	6636	349.26	39	79	32	1.68	28/02/2014
G "A Harzing"...	223	6727	354.05	39	79	33	1.74	01/04/2014
G "A Harzing"...	224	6825	359.21	39	80	33	1.74	03/05/2014
G "A Harzing"...	225	6915	363.95	40	80	33	1.74	02/06/2014
G "A Harzing"...	234	7113	374.37	40	82	34	1.79	02/07/2014
G "A Harzing"...	236	7191	378.47	40	82	34	1.79	01/08/2014
G "A Harzing"...	235	7330	385.79	40	83	34	1.79	03/09/2014
G "A Harzing"...	234	7395	389.21	40	83	34	1.79	03/10/2014
G "A Harzing"...	243	7506	395.05	41	84	34	1.79	01/11/2014
G "A Harzing"...	248	7641	402.16	41	85	35	1.84	30/11/2014
G "A Harzing"...	249	7742	387.10	41	85	35	1.75	01/01/2015
G "A Harzing"...	253	8103	405.15	42	87	35	1.75	01/02/2015
G "A Harzing"...	253	8230	411.50	42	88	35	1.75	04/03/2015
G "A Harzing"...	253	8356	417.80	42	89	35	1.75	01/04/2015
G "A Harzing"...	255	8467	423.35	42	89	35	1.75	30/04/2015
G "A Harzing"...	259	8638	431.90	42	90	35	1.75	01/06/2015
G "A Harzing"...	244	8913	445.65	44	92	35	1.75	02/07/2015
G "A Harzing"...	245	9041	452.05	44	93	36	1.80	01/08/2015
G "A Harzing"...	248	9117	455.85	44	93	36	1.80	03/09/2015
G "A Harzing"...	250	9203	460.15	44	94	36	1.80	03/10/2015
G "A Harzing"...	251	9309	465.45	44	94	36	1.80	03/11/2015
G "A Harzing"...	250	9430	471.50	44	95	36	1.80	04/12/2015

Longitudinal searches for growth of research area

However, longitudinal searches can also serve many other purposes, such as the growth of publications in a particular research area or the development of impact of particular journals over time.

Longitudinal data illustrate differences in research metrics

Longitudinal data also allow us to illustrate the features of different research metrics. In the author example above, you can clearly see how the number of citations increases quite rapidly. In contrast, the h-index, the g-index and the hI,norm increase at a slow but steady rate. The number of citations per year also increases, but takes a small dip every January when the year is increased by 1.

hI,annual metrics tends to be fairly stable over time

In contrast, the hI,annual is quite stable over time, dipping every January when the year is increased by 1, gradually rising again over the year as the hI,norm increases and then dipping again in January. This show clearly that it is very hard to substantially increase the hI,annual and that even maintaining it needs a steady increase in the hI,norm to counteract the natural decline over the years.

PoP tip 34: Multi-query center (10): Aggregating queries

The Publish or Perish **Multi-query center** also makes it possible to aggregate queries at a higher level of aggregation in just two simple steps and less than 20 seconds.

Why would you want to aggregate queries?

There might be a number of key scenarios in which you might want to aggregate queries

Aggregate academic metrics across a research group or department.

Calculating metrics at the level of a research group, department, or school after searching for individual **academics** in that entity. As Google Scholar does not have a reliable affiliation search, this is the only way to assess the collective performance of a group of researchers.

Aggregate article metrics across a research group or department

Calculating metrics at the level of a research group, department, or school after searching for individual **articles** published by that entity.

Metrics for a collection of articles

Calculating the metrics for **any collection of articles** of interest. For instance one might want to assess the collective impact of a specific set of articles in a particular field of research.

Combine results of split-year searches for one journal

Combining the results of a number of **identical** journal queries split up by year to address the Google Scholar 1,000 results limit. This would allow you to get a comprehensive record of publications in most journals as few have more than 1,000 publications a year.

Combine results of different journal searches

Combining the results of a number of **different** queries that could not be combined into a single query because of Google Scholar limitations in field size. For instance one might want to search for articles on a specific topic in a range of journals, but Google Scholar's journal field only allows a certain number of characters.

Worked example: Institutional aggregation

Let's assume we want to assess the performance of the Department of Management & Marketing at the University of Melbourne (my previous employer). The screenshot below show the query results for all 15 full professors in the department, sorted by h-index. We then select all queries and right-click to get the pop-up menu (see Using PoP). Select **Save as CSV...** and give the file a meaningful name.

Query	Papers	Cites	Cites/year	h	g	hI,norm	hI,annual
"Cynthia Hardy" from...	209	18525	578.91	58	135	48	1.50
"A Harzing", NOT ivor...	252	9499	474.95	44	95	36	1.80
"Danny Samson" OR "...	197	6707	209.59	30	81	21	0.66
				45		17	1.06
				53		19	1.06
				58		16	0.80
				47		14	0.61
				51		15	0.60
				33		12	0.80
				24		12	0.92
				31		11	0.65
				33		10	0.59
				22		11	0.29
				20		9	0.36
				22		9	0.38

Menu:

Lookup	Ctrl+L
Lookup Direct	Ctrl+Shift+L
Mark for Lookup	
Recalculate Metrics	
New Query...	Ctrl+N
New Folder...	Ctrl+Shift+N
New Import...	Ctrl+O
Save As BibTeX...	
Save As CSV...	Ctrl+S

Subsequently, simply re-import this file into PoP. The screenshot below shows the resulting data, sorted by hI,annual. Combined, the department's professors have an h-index of 119, and more than 56,000 citations.

Find the Department's most cited articles

Having the complete list of the Department's academic articles also allows one to assess which are the Department's most highly cited articles, both overall and per year, which journals its academics publish in etc.

Multi-query center - Manage and compare multiple citation queries

Query	Source	Papers	Cites	Cites/year	h	g	hI,norm	hI,annual
Melbourne DOMM Profe...	Publish or Perish (CSV)	1475	56676	1491.47	119	219	84	2.21
"A Harzing", NOT ivoren...	Google Scholar	252	9499	474.95	44	95	36	1.80
"Cynthia Hardy" from 19...	Google Scholar	209	18525	578.91	58	135	48	1.50
"Simon J Bell" from 1999...	Google Scholar	45	3339	208.69	23	45	17	1.06
"Damien Power": all	Google Scholar	99	2818	156.56	23	53	19	1.06
"Dean Xu", NOT "XJLSY ...	Google Scholar	24	1450	111.54	15	24	12	0.92
"Bryan Lukas": all	Google Scholar	70	3438	171.90	21	58	16	0.80
"Jane W Lu", NOT cance...	Google Scholar	33	2216	147.73	16	33	12	0.80
"Danny Samson" OR "Da...	Google Scholar	197	6707	209.59	30	81	21	0.66
"Michelle Brown", NOT "...	Google Scholar	59	1047	61.59	15	31	11	0.65
"Bill Harley": all	Google Scholar	88	2277	99.00	20	47	14	0.61

All queries
- Recent queries
- Older queries
- A-Archive
  - ABS conference
  - AoM presidents
  - DOMM benchma
    - Google Schola
      - Level B
      - Level C
      - Level D
      - Level E

Results

Papers:	1475	Cites/paper:	38.42	h-index:	119	Melbourne DOMM Professors.csv [2015-12-17 12:27:16]
Citations:	56676	Cites/author:	29636.30	g-index:	219	Query date: 2015-12-17
Years:	38	Papers/author:	854.82	hI,norm:	84	Papers: 1475
Cites/year:	1491.47	Authors/paper:	2.26	hI,annual:	2.21	Citations: 56676
						Years: 38

Cites	Per year	Authors	Title	Year
h 1614	124.15	N Phillips, C Hardy	Discourse analysis: Investigating processes of social construction	2002
h 1258	78.63	D Samson, M Terziovski	The relationship between total quality management practices and operational performance	1999
h 1157	105.18	S Maguire, C Hardy, TB Lawrence	Institutional entrepreneurship in emerging fields: HIV/AIDS treatment advocacy in Canada	2004
h 1111	101.00	N Phillips, TB Lawrence, C Hardy	Discourse and institutions	2004
h 1062	55.89	D Dougherty, C Hardy	Sustained product innovation in large, mature organizations: Overcoming innovation-to-or...	1996

63

Worked example: Aggregation of collection of articles

This screenshot shows the results of an aggregation of 230 articles related to the role of language in international business. We used this for a review article on this topic.

Multi-query center - Manage and compare multiple citation queries

	Query	Source	Papers	Cites	Cites/year	h	g	hI,norm	hI,annual
All queries									
Recent queries	Language Review Articles.csv ...	Publish or Perish (CSV)	230	9526	250.68	55	90	42	1.11
Older queries	A communication-based the...	Google Scholar	1	25	6.25	1	1	1	0.25
A-Archive	A linguistic and philosophical...	Google Scholar	1	2	2.00	1	1	1	1.00
A-Harzing longitudin	A more expansive perspective...	Google Scholar	1	1	1.00	1	1	1	1.00
A-Old research proje	A research paradigm for inter...	Google Scholar	1	26	2.60	1	1	1	0.10

Results

Papers:	230	Cites/paper:	41.42	h-index:	55	Language Review Articles.csv [2015-12-17 15:10:37]
Citations:	9526	Cites/author:	5609.61	g-index:	90	Query date: 2015-12-17
Years:	38	Papers/author:	140.27	hI,norm:	42	Papers: 230
Cites/year:	250.68	Authors/paper:	2.03	hI,annual:	1.11	Citations: 9526
						Years: 38

Cites	Per year	Authors	Title	Year
h 340	21.25	R Marschan-Piekkari, D Welch, L Welch	In the shadow: The impact of language on structure, power and communication in the multinational	1999
h 292	41.71	J Melitz	Language and foreign trade	2008
h 261	14.50	R Marschan, D Welch, L Welch	Language: The forgotten factor in multinational management	1997
h 239	23.90	L Louhiala-Salminen, M Charles	English as a lingua franca in Nordic corporate mergers: Two case companies	2005
h 237	19.75	AJ Feely, AW Harzing	Language management in multinational companies	2003
h 209	9.95	BH Schmitt, Y Pan, NT Tavassoli	Language and consumer memory: The impact of linguistic differences between Chinese and English	1994
h 199	19.90	C Nickerson	English as a lingua franca in international business contexts	2005
h 199	19.90	E Vaara, J Tienari, R Piekkari	Language and the circuits of power in a merging multinational corporation	2005
h 181	13.92	C Welch, R Marschan-Piekkari, H Pent...	Corporate elites as informants in qualitative international business research	2002
h 178	25.43	AW Harzing, AJ Feely	The language barrier and its implications for HQ-subsidiary relationships	2008

Worked example: Journal aggregation

A journal like *Scientometrics* publishes a large number of articles per year. Hence a search without year limitations will always run into the Google Scholar limitation of 1,000 results. Thus low cited articles will not show up in your searches. If you wanted to have a complete record of articles published in *Scientometrics* for the last 10 years, you could run five searches for 2006-2007, 2008-2009, 2010-2011, 2012-2013 and 2014-2015 and then combine them into one file (see screenshot).

Multi-query center - Manage and compare multiple citation queries

	Query	Source	Papers	Cites	Cites/year	h	g	hI,norm	hI,annual
A-Old research proje	"Scientometrics" from 2014 to 2015: all	Google Scholar	746	2359	2359.00	19	27	11	11.00
ERC Advanced Grant	"Scientometrics" from 2012 to 2013: all	Google Scholar	428	4409	1469.67	27	35	18	6.00
HROB	"Scientometrics" from 2010 to 2011: all	Google Scholar	502	11435	2287.00	47	69	32	6.40
Institutions	"Scientometrics" from 2008 to 2009: all	Google Scholar	360	10671	1524.43	50	78	37	5.29
Language review	"Scientometrics" from 2006 to 2007: all	Google Scholar	301	15158	1684.22	63	109	44	4.89
PoP Blog	Scientometrics 2006-2015.csv [2015-1...	Publish or Perish (CSV)	2337	44032	4892.44	82	130	57	6.33
Satu project									

Results

Papers:	2337	Cites/paper:	18.84	h-index:	82	Scientometrics 2006-2015.csv [2015-12-17 16:11:00]
Citations:	44032	Cites/author:	24535.31	g-index:	130	Query date: 2015-12-17
Years:	9	Papers/author:	1220.26	hI,norm:	57	Papers: 2337
Cites/year:	4892.44	Authors/paper:	2.53	hI,annual:	6.33	Citations: 44032
						Years: 9

Cites	Per year	Rank	Authors	Title	Year	Publication
h 1204	133.78	1	L Egghe	Theory and practise of the g-index	2006	Scientometrics
h 523	58.11	2	AFJ Van Raan	Comparison of the Hirsch-index with standard bibliometric indicators and with ...	2006	scientometrics
h 475	52.78	3	T Braun, W Glanzel, A Schubert	A Hirsch-type index for journals	2006	Scientometrics
h 430	61.43	1	J Bar-Ilan	Which h-index?—A comparison of WoS, Scopus and Google Scholar	2008	Scientometrics
h 421	46.78	4	PD Batista, MG Campiteli, O Kinouchi	Is it possible to compare researchers with different scientific interests?	2006	Scientometrics
h 404	44.89	5	AJ Nederhof	Bibliometric monitoring of research performance in the social sciences and the...	2006	Scientometrics
h 315	39.38	6	A Sidiropoulos, D Katsaros, Y Manolop...	Generalized Hirsch h-index for disclosing latent facts in citation networks	2007	Scientometrics
h 305	50.83	3	N van Eck, L Waltman	Software survey: VOSviewer, a computer program for bibliometric mapping	2009	Scientometrics
h 300	50.00	2	A Porter, I Rafols	Is science becoming more interdisciplinary? Measuring and mapping six resear...	2009	Scientometrics
h 300	60.00	1	I Rafols, M Meyer	Diversity and network coherence as indicators of interdisciplinarity: case stud...	2010	Scientometrics

This allows you to compare the more than 2,300 papers published in the journal in the last decade, rather than focusing only on the 1,000 most cited ones. This is especially important for more recent articles, as these are likely to fall outside the top 1,000 if one conducts an aggregate search for 2006-2015.

PoP tip 35: Accuracy: PoP does NOT give results that are different from Google Scholar

Contrary to what some users think, PoP does **not** give results that are different from Google Scholar! Publish or Perish is as accurate or as inaccurate as Google Scholar itself.

PoP vs. GS: Same search gives the same results

If you conduct the **same** search in Publish or Perish as in Google Scholar, you will get the **same** result. We do not perform any magic or make adjustments to your record!

PoP vs. GS: Different results caused by different search

If the Publish or Perish results differ from the ones you get by using Google Scholar directly, this is typically caused by the fact that Publish or Perish uses the **Advanced Scholar Search** capabilities of Google Scholar, whereas your manual search probably used the standard Google Scholar search.

The latter is equivalent to an **All of the words** search, which matches the search terms **anywhere** in the searched documents (author, title, source, abstract, references etc.) and usually provides far too many irrelevant results for an effective citation analysis.

Worked example: standard search vs. author search

If you would for instance search for my name using the standard Google Scholar search (i.e. **All of the words**) rather than the author search, you would get more than 1,000 papers and more than 40,000 citations (see screenshot). Instead an author search for "harzing a" results in "just" 300 papers and 9500 citations.

General citation search - Perform a general citation search

Author(s):

Publication:

All of the words: "harzing a"

Any of the words:

None of the words:

The phrase:

Year of publication between: and: 0   ☐ Title words only

Data source: Google Scholar ▼

Results

Papers:	1000	Papers/author:	593.24	h-index:	97	"harzing a": all
Citations:	40890	Cites/year:	1703.75	g-index:	170	Query date: 2015-12-05
Years:	24	Cites/auth/year:	1031.58	hc-index:	72	Papers: 1000
Cites/paper:	40.89	hI,annual:	2.92	hI,norm:	70	Citations: 40890
						Years: 24

Cites	Per year	Rank	Authors	Title
☑ h 1356	271.20	622	T Blaschke	Object based image analysis for remote sensing
☑ h 983	983.00	184	RF Fellows, AMM Liu	Research methods for construction
☑ h 792	79.20	145	A Riege	Three-dozen knowledge-sharing barriers managers must consider
☑ h 674	74.89	314	CE Lance, MM Butts, LC Michels	The sources of four commonly reported cutoff criteria what did they really say?
☑ h 610	55.45	277	M Hess	'Spatial'relationships? Towards a reconceptualization of embedded ness
☑ h 594	59.40	375	L Tihanyi, DA Griffith...	The effect of cultural distance on entry mode choice, international diversification,
☑ h 480	53.33	372	FJ Acedo, C Barroso, JL Galan	The resource-based theory: dissemination and main trends
☑ h 476	34.00	148	P Dicken, A Malmberg	Firms in territories: A relational perspective*
☑ h 450	34.62	2	AW Harzing	Acquisitions versus greenfield investments: International strategy and manageme

The **all of the words** search matches "harzing a" anywhere in the document, including all articles citing my work that appear in full-text in Google Scholar and where "harzing a" appears in the reference list. Please note that the order does matter in the **All of the words** field, so we search for "harzing a", not "a harzing", as references will usually reproduce author names as "family name, initial". As you can see, the first 8 papers in the results were not authored by me.

Google scholar rank differs from citation rank

In the above screenshot the resulting papers are ordered by the number of citations, not by Google Scholar rank, which is the standard ranking for a general search. As you can see in the rank column, articles that are less relevant (i.e. that do not have my name in a prominent field, such as the author field) have a low Google Scholar rank (145-622), whereas the first paper that is authored by me has a high Google Scholar rank (#2)

Want to replicate standard Google Scholar search in Publish or Perish?

If you really **do** want to get the same results in Publish or Perish as with a standard Google Scholar search, do the following.

1. Go to the General citation search page.
2. Empty all text fields except **All of the words**.
3. Enter your query terms in the **All of the words** field.
4. Set the Year of publication fields both to 0.
5. Clear the Title words only field.
6. Click on Lookup.
7. When the results appear, click on the Rank column header to sort the results in the order in which Google Scholar returned them.

PoP tip 36: Improve author search accuracy (1): Check whether the years make sense

It is advisable to check the **Years** result in Publish or Perish to see whether it reflects common sense.

Year values that are too high

Obviously, if the value is >100 for an author, something is wrong. However, even finding values of >40 for authors should lead you to be suspicious, unless the academic is close to retirement.

Sort results by year

As my last name (Harzing) is fairly unique and there are no other academics with the same last name that publish regularly, I often tend to conduct Publish or Perish searches with my last name only (see screenshot). However, this leads to a **Years** value of 62, which is clearly impossible. Sorting by year easily allows me to spot the offending publications.

Author impact analysis - Perform a citation analysis for one or more authors

Author's name:	harzing						
Exclude these names:							
Year of publication between:		and:					
Data source:	Google Scholar	▼					

Results

Papers:	267	Papers/author:	192.30	h-index:	44	harzing: all	
Citations:	9467	Cites/year:	152.69	g-index:	95	Query date: 2015-12-05	
Years:	62	Cites/auth/year:	113.09	hc-index:	41	Papers: 267 Citations: 9467	
Cites/paper:	35.46	hI,annual:	0.58	hI,norm:	36	Years: 62	

Cites		Per year	Authors	Title	Year	Publication
☑	0	0.00	W Harzing	Het kleine Driebergen	1953	Maandblad van" Oud-Utrecht", jg. 26 (1953), no. …
☑	1	0.02	W Harzing	Rijsenburg jubileerde in 1835	1956	Maandblad van" Oud-Utrecht", jg. 29 (1956), no. 1, …
☑	0	0.00	W Harzing	De Driebergse Traaij in 1777, 1812 en 1817	1957	Maandblad van Oud-Utrecht, jg. 30 (1957), nr. 11, …
☑	0	0.00	W Harzing	Het station Driebergen-Zeist	1963	Maandblad van Oud-Utrecht, jg. 36 (1963), nr. 2, p. …
☑	1	0.02	W Harzing	Het raadhuis" Sparrendaal" vroeger en nu	1964	Maandblad van Oud-Utrecht, jg. 37 (1964), nr. 4, p. …
☑	2	0.04	W Harzing	De riddermatige hofstede en ambachtsheerlijkheid Rijsenburg	1967	Jaarboekje van" Oud-Utrecht
☑	0	0.00	W Harzing	De plattegrond van het kasteel Rijsenburg	1967	Maandblad van Oud-Utrecht, jg. 40 (1967), nr. 8, p. …
☑	2	0.05	W Harzing	Driebergen en Rijsenburg: Hoe zij ontstonden en groeiden	1973	
☑ h	345	17.25	AWK Harzing	The persistent myth of high expatriate failure rates	1995	International Journal of Human Resource …
☑	44	2.20	M Borg, AW Harzing	Composing an international staff	1995	International human resource management
☑	15	0.75	AW Harzing	Strategic planning in multinational corporations	1995	International human resource management
☑	1	0.05	AW Harzing	Research Note An International Bibliography	1995	European Journal of Industrial Relations
☑ h	98	5.16	AW Harzing, G Hofstede	Planned change in organizations: The influence of national culture	1996	Research in the Sociology of Organizations

Remove publications from a namesake from an earlier generation

The first eight publications are historical articles and books by my late grandfather (Wim Harzing) about the city in which he lived. Hence sorting by year is also a very good way to separate your own publications from those of a namesake from an earlier generation.

Ensuring a reasonable "academic age"

Sorting by year can also be used to ensure that any metrics based on "academic age" (i.e. the number of years since your first publication) are a reasonable reflection of the academic's career. If for instance you find that someone has published one article in a fairly obscure journal (maybe in another language) or published a master's thesis many years before a steady stream of articles emerged, it might be justifiable to simply exclude this publication from the analysis.

Sorting by year to spot Google Scholar parsing errors

Sorting by year is also a good way to spot Google Scholar parsing errors where Google Scholar has mistakenly interpreted numbers elsewhere in the article as the year of publication.

PoP tip 37: Improve author search accuracy (2): Merge duplicate citations

For most authors you will notice duplicate or near-duplicate articles in the Publish or Perish Results list. These duplicates may be due to one or more of the following:

- Sloppy referencing. Not all references to an author's work are accurate. Small differences in the names of the authors, the article's title, or its source may cause the same article to appear more than once.
- Google Scholar parsing the publication from more than one source.

Non standard publications have more duplicates

The former will happen more often with publications that are of a "non-standard" format, such as books, book chapters, conference papers, and software as – unlike journal articles – there is no universally agreed way to reference them. Publish or Perish itself for instance is referenced in more than thirty different ways.

✓	h	304	38.00	AW Harzing	Publish or perish
✓	4	0.80		AW Harzing	Publish or Perish (Version 2.8), software program
✓	4	0.50		AW Harzing	Publish or perish (Version 3.2)[Software]
✓	2	0.25		AW Harzing	Publish or perish (Version 3.6)[Computer software]
✓	4	0.50		AW Harzing	Publish or perish [Computer software]
✓	2	0.00		AW HARZING	Publish or Perish [on-line]. 2007 [Dostęp 02.05. 2012]
✓	5	1.00		AW Harzing	Publish or perish [software program](Version 2.8)
✓	3	0.38		AW Harzing	Publish or Perish 2.0
✓	4	1.00		AW Harzing	Publish or Perish 3.1
✓	2	0.25		AW Harzing	Publish or Perish Version 2.0. 2673 (Software)
✓	2	0.29		AW Harzing	Publish or perish version 2.5. 2969 (software)
✓	2	0.00		A Harzing	Publish or Perish, 2010: version 3.0
✓	2	0.25		AW Harzing	Publish or Perish, revisado 27 de noviembre 2011
✓	3	0.38		AW Harzing	Publish or Perish, ver. 2, 2007
✓	6	0.86		AWK Harzing	Publish or Perish, version 2.5. 3171
✓	8	1.60		AW Harzing	Publish or Perish, version 2.8
✓	3	0.60		AW Harzing	Publish or Perish, version 2.8. 3644; 2010
✓	25	6.25		AW Harzing	Publish or Perish, version 3
✓	3	0.60		AW Harzing	Publish or perish, version 3.0. 3869
✓	2	0.40		AW Harzing	Publish or perish, version 3.0. 3883 (18 August 2010)
✓	5	1.25		A Harzing	Publish or Perish, version 3.1. 4004
✓	2	0.50		AW Harzing	Publish or perish, version 3.2. 4150
✓	21	21.00		AW Harzing	Publish or perish. 2007
✓	3	0.75		AW Harzing	Publish or Perish. 2011
✓	2	0.25		AW Harzing	Publish or Perish. Retrieved April 25, 2012
✓	2	0.25		AW Harzing	Publish or perish. Retrieved from h ttp
✓	5	1.00		A Harzing	Publish or perish. Retrieved on September 6, 2010
✓	3	0.60		AW Harzing	Publish or Perish. Version 3.0. 3813
✓	2	2.00		AW HARZING	Publish or perish.[sn] 2007
✓	5	0.71		AW Harzing	Publish or Perish: A citation analysis software program
✓	3	0.38		AW Harzing	Publish or Perish[Software program]

A white paper on my web-site has three different records.

	13	2.60	AW Harzing	Citation analysis across disciplines: The Impact of different data sources and citation metrics
	2	0.40	AW Harzing	Citation analysis across disciplines: The impact of different data sources and citation metrics (2010)
	3	1.00	A Harzing	Citation analysis across disciplines: the impact of different data sources and citation metrics. Retrieved August 1, 2013

Effect of duplicates on citation analysis

The effect on the citation analysis is that:

- The total number of articles may come out higher than the actual number, because duplicates are counted separately.
- The citations per paper may come out lower, for the same reason.
- The h-index and g-index may come out differently, because citations are spread over the duplicates.

Merge duplicates by simple drag and drop

Since Version 3.0 of Publish or Perish, duplicates can be merged into the master record, simply by dragging the stray citation onto the master record. The merged record of the white paper above is shown in the screenshot below.

	h	90	11.25	JB Hocking, ...	Balancing global and local strategic contexts: Expatriate knowledge transfer, applications, and learning within a trans.
		28	14.00	AW Harzing...	Challenges in international survey research: a review with illustrations and suggested solutions for best practice
		18	3.60	AW Harzing	Citation analysis across disciplines: The Impact of different data sources and citation metrics
	h	67	9.57	A Josiassen...	Comment: Descending from the ivory tower: reflections on the relevance and future of country-of-origin research

PoP tip 38: Improve author search accuracy (3): Selective merging around the h-index cut-off

Selective merging in Publish or Perish saves time if you are only interested in the h-index.

Check publications that are "just out" of the h-index

This involves checking whether you have any publications that are close to becoming part of the h-index and verify whether any stray references can be found for those. These references can then be merged into their master record. I would normally recommend checking all publications within 5 citations of reaching the required number of citations to be included in the h-index.

Extended example of selective merge

Let's work through an example of how this works. The screenshot below shows the publications in my "raw" citation record - back in 2009 - that might qualify for inclusion in the h-index. The Expatriate Failure article with Christensen is the last paper to be included in my then h-index of 23.

☑	25	5.00	AW Harzing, N Noorder...	Knowledge flows in MNCs: an empirical test and extension of Gupta and C
☑	24	3.43	AW Harzing, C Christen...	Expatriate failure: time to abandon the concept?
☑	21	4.20	AW Harzing	Response styles in cross-national survey research: A 26-country study
☑	21	4.20	AW Harzing	Response styles in cross-national survey research
☑	21	2.33	AW Harzing, M Maznevski	The interaction between language and culture: A test of the cultural accc
☑	20	5.00	AW Harzing	Publish or perish
☑	18	2.57	AW Harzing	Journal quality list

Duplicate paper without sub-title

The next paper [*Response styles in cross-national survey research*] has 21 citations, but there is a duplicate paper with an equal number of citations. The duplicate paper does not include the subtitle, but a quick verification of the citing articles shows that they are indeed different from those citing the paper with the subtitle. Hence this would be a prime candidate for merging, which increases the h-index to 24.

Merging doesn't always increase the h-index

The next paper [*The interaction between language and culture*] does have some stray citations (found by sorting the results by publication), but not enough to enter into the h-index. The Publish or Perish program has a fairly large number of stray citations with academics referring to different versions, and hence when merged becomes part of the h-index with 26 citations. However, as the original last paper included [Expatriate Failure:...] only has 24 citations, the h-index still remains at 24. Checking this paper, however, I also found some stray citations. Merging them into the master record results in an h-index of 25. The Journal quality list also has stray citations, but not enough to bring the total up to 26.

Merging duplicates can also decrease the h-index

However, in this process I also noticed that one my most-cited publications – the book **Managing the Multinationals** – actually appears twice. It appears once with a subtitle and 160 citations and once without a subtitle and 37 citations, thus contributing to the h-index twice. Obviously, these two titles need to be merged, bringing us back to an h-index of 24.

Selective merge only takes a few minutes

Although this whole process sounds fairly involved, with a little practice it can actually be done in a couple of minutes, whereas a full merge of stray citations can easily take 15-20 minutes. Hence selective merging might be a good compromise.

Generic lessons for selective merging

This process has also taught us two important generic lessons for selective merging:

- Publications with subtitles can often appear twice, once with and once without the subtitle, so it is worthwhile to check them.
- Your most highly cited publications might appear in the h-index twice if the number of stray citations is large enough to enter as a separate publication.

PoP tip 39: What the heck are all these metrics (1)?
Simple metrics

Although most bibliometric analyses tend to focus on fairly complex metrics such as the h-index and its variations, there is a lot one can learn from relatively simple metrics included in Publish or Perish.

Metrics related to papers, citations and academic age

Here we look at the number of papers, citations, and the number of years since the academic's first publication, in combination with the number of authors per paper.

- **Citations per paper** = total citations/total papers
- **Citations per year** = total citations/years since first paper
- **Citations per author** = divide citations for each publication by the number of authors and sum the resulting citations; this is the single-authored equivalent number of citations for the author in question.
- **Papers per author** = divide each publication by the number of authors and sum the fractional author counts; this is the single-authored equivalent number of papers for the author in question.
- **Authors per paper** = add up the total number of authors involved in the publications for the author in question and divide this by the number of papers. *[Please note: Single publications with a large number of authors can increase this metric substantially. Hence, it is not as good a reflection of an author's individual productivity as the number of papers per author.]*

What can we learn from simple metrics?

The screenshots below compare my own publication record (left) with that of a former colleague at the University of Melbourne, Maria Kraimer (right), now Professor at the University of Iowa. For both I have merged duplicate publications.

Results

Papers:	111	Cites/paper:	85.56
Citations:	9497	Cites/author:	7043.05
Years:	20	Papers/author:	73.15
Cites/year:	474.85	Authors/paper:	1.86

Results

Papers:	41	Cites/paper:	202.54
Citations:	8304	Cites/author:	2779.79
Years:	17	Papers/author:	14.37
Cites/year:	488.47	Authors/paper:	3.17

I chose Maria because her total number of citations (app. 8300) and time since first publication (17 years) are quite similar to mine (app. 9500 and 20 years). As a result, our number of citations per year is very similar (475 vs. 488).

Different publication strategies

However, it is clear that we have followed different publication strategies. I have published more than 2.5 times as many papers (111 vs. 41). An important reason is that she has focused mainly on publications in top US journals, whilst I have published in a wider range of journals.

I have also published books and book chapters as well as white papers and other research products (such as Publish or Perish and the Journal Quality List) that attract citations. As a result the number of citations per paper is much higher for Maria (202.54) than for me (85.56). This could be seen as evidence of publishing higher quality papers.

Differences in co-authorship patterns

However, Maria has also published with a much larger number of co-authors. As a result, my number of "single-authored" citations (cites/author) is 2.5 times as high as hers. The difference in the number of single-authored equivalent papers is even larger, with my record showing more than 5 times as many single-authored equivalents (73 papers vs. 14 papers).

This is also reflected in the average number of authors per paper. For Maria the mean is 3.17, whereas for me it is 1.86. This difference is not as large as one might expect from the other metrics, but single papers with many co-authors can heavily influence this metric. Publish or Perish therefore also provides the mode for this metric. For Maria the mode is 3, whereas for me the mode is 1 (i.e. single-authored).

Conclusion

Neither of these two publication strategies is inherently better than the other. They just reflect different approaches to publishing, which might be shaped by factors such as type and country of doctoral training, country of employment, research area, and personal temperaments.

The variety of metrics provided by Publish or Perish allows one to select the metrics most appropriate to one's purpose. However, there are metrics that are designed to combine both productivity (number of papers) and impact (number of citations). The h-index, to be discussed next, is the most important of these metrics.

PoP tip 40: What the heck are all these metrics (2)? H and G index

Publish or Perish provides a wide range of metrics. The most important ones are listed in the most right-hand column of the results list. Here we explain the two most influential of them and then provide an illustration based on the same academics as before.

h-index

Unless you have been hiding under a stone in the last ten years, you will probably have heard about the h-index. It is defined as follows (Hirsch, 2005:16569):

> *A scientist has index h if h of his/her Np papers have at least h citations each, and the other (Np-h) papers have no more than h citations each.*

A h-index of 20 means that an academic has published at least 20 papers that have received at least 20 citations each. The h-index thus combines an assessment of both quantity (number of papers) and an approximation of quality (impact, or citations to these papers).

h-index rewards consistent stream of high-impact publications

An academic cannot have a high h-index without publishing a substantial number of papers. However, this is not enough. These papers need to be cited in order to count for the h-index. Hence the h-index favours academics that publish a continuous stream of papers with lasting and above-average impact.

- Hirsch, J. E. (15 November 2005). *"An index to quantify an individual's scientific research output". PNAS* **102** (46): 16569–16572.

g-index

The g-index is calculated based on the distribution of citations received by a given researcher's publications, such that:

> *given a set of articles ranked in decreasing order of the number of citations that they received, the g-index is the unique largest number such that the top g articles received together at least g^2 citations.*

g-index looks at overall record

A g-index of 20 means that and academic has published at least 20 articles that **combined** have received at least 400 citations. However, unlike the h-index these citations could be generated by only a small number of articles. For instance an academic with 20 papers, 15 of which have no citations with the remaining five having respectively 350, 35, 10, 3 and 2 citations would have a g-index of 20, but a h-index of 3 (three papers with at least 3 citations each).

g-index allows highly-cited papers to bolster low-cited papers

Roughly, *h* is the number of papers of a certain "quality" [citations] threshold, a threshold that rises as h rises; *g* allows citations from higher-cited papers to be used to bolster lower-cited papers in meeting this threshold. Therefore, in all cases g is at least h, and is in most cases higher. However, unlike the h-index, the g-index saturates whenever the average number of citations for all published papers exceeds the total number of published papers; the way it is defined, the g-index is not adapted to this situation.

- Egghe, Leo (2006) Theory and practise of the g-index, Scientometrics, vol. 69, No 1, pp. 131–152. doi:10.1007/s11192-006-0144-7

What can one conclude from complex metrics?

Here I return to the publication records of Maria and myself. As indicated earlier, our total number of citations (approximately 8300 vs. 9500) and time since first publication are quite similar (17 years vs. 20 years). As a result, our number of citations per year is very similar too (489 vs. 475). This time I show the more complex metrics. What can we conclude from these?

h-index:	45	h-index:	26
g-index:	97	g-index:	41
hI,norm:	37	hI,norm:	21
hI,annual:	1.85	hI,annual:	1.24

h-index

My record shows a higher h-index than that of Maria. This is not surprising, given that she has published fewer papers and hence it is more difficult for her to achieve a high h-index. In Maria's case, only one third of her papers are *not* included in the h-index. In my case, this is true for nearly 60% of my papers. That said, given that her h-index is lower, it is easier for her to increase it further as her next paper only needs to acquire 27 citations to be included, whereas my next paper needs to acquire 46 citations.

g-index

My g-index is more than twice as high as that of Maria. The simple reason is that neither the g-index nor the h-index can be higher than the total number of papers published and Maria has "only" published 41 papers so far. Hence, the maximum her g-index can reach is 41. Even if she would publish another paper without any citations, her g-index would still increase. This is clearly a limitation of the g-index.

Conclusions

The h-index and g-index are both limited by the number of papers one publishes. Hence these indices – and especially the g-index – will always favour academics that publish more papers (provided they are cited at least moderately well). These indices are therefore not very suitable to assess the impact of academics that have published one or two groundbreaking contributions, but have not published any further highly cited work. For these academics, the total number of citations might be a more appropriate metric. That's exactly why Publish or Perish provides a wide range of metrics. The variety of metrics allows you to select the metrics most appropriate to your purpose.

PoP tip 41: What the heck are all these metrics (3)?
hI,norm and hI,annual

In the last decade, the h-index has become a very popular tool to compare academics. Unfortunately, it has two major drawbacks.

1. Large differences in h-index between disciplines

First, there are large differences in typical h-values between disciplines. Part of these disciplinary differences are caused by the fact that academics in the Life Sciences and Sciences typically publish more (and shorter) articles. They also typically publish with a larger number of co-authors than academics in the Social Sciences and Humanities.

2. Large differences in h-index between junior and senior academics

Second, the h-index is a less appropriate measure of academic achievement for junior academics, as their papers have not yet had the time to accumulate citations. Especially in the Social Sciences and Humanities it might take more than five years before a paper acquires a significant number of citations.

Introducing two new metrics: hI,norm and hIa

The two remaining statistics in the most right-hand column of the Publish or Perish results section - hI,norm and hIa - are metrics that I introduced to address the problem of disciplinary and career stage differences. These two metrics "correct" for differences in the number of co-authorships and for differences in academic age. As such they are more suitable for comparisons across disciplines and career stages.

hI,norm

The hI,norm is an individual h-index. The hI,norm is calculated as follows:

- normalize the number of citations for each paper by dividing the number of citations by the number of authors for that paper, and then calculate the h-index of the *normalized* citation counts

Those with co-authors can achieve the same hI,norm

Someone who co-publishes with others will not need to publish more articles to achieve the same hI,norm as an academic who publishes single-authored articles. However, the co-authored articles will need to gather more citations to become part of the hI,norm, as the article's citations will be divided by the number of co-authors.

Illustrating the hI,norm

h-index:	45	h-index:	44	h-index:	23	h-index:	18
g-index:	97	g-index:	79	g-index:	67	g-index:	53
hI,norm:	37	hI,norm:	20	hI,norm:	20	hI,norm:	18
hI,annual:	1.85	hI,annual:	0.91	hI,annual:	0.67	hI,annual:	0.45

The example above shows how academics with the same h-index can have very different individual h-indices (hI,norm). The first screenshot shows my own record, an academic in the Social Sciences with a substantial number of single-authored articles. The second screenshot presents a Professor in Physics at the University of Melbourne, with a similar h-index, but a much lower hI,norm as most of his articles were co-authored with at least three other academics.

The third and fourth screenshot show two other Professors at the same University (in the Social Sciences and Humanities) who had a similar hI,norm as the Physics Professor with much lower h-indices as their work was largely (or solely) single-authored.

hI,annual (hIa)

The hI,annual (hIa for short) addresses the problem of comparing academics at different career stages. It is calculated as follows:
- *hIa*: hI,norm/academic age, where:
  - academic age: number of years elapsed since first publication

hI, annual = number single-author equivalent impactful articles per year

The hIa-index thus measures the average number of single-author equivalent h-index points that an academic has accumulated in *each* year of their academic career. A hIa of 1.0 means that an academic has *consistently* published one article per year that, when corrected for the number of co-authors, has accumulated enough citations to be included in the h-index. The three last academics in the hI,norm example above have very different hI,annual indices, despite having similar hI,norm indices because their academic age runs from 22 to 40.

Illustrating the hI,annual

Below, I have reproduced the metrics of four high-performing individuals at different career stages. They have respectively been publishing for 9, 20, 29 and 40 years. As is immediately obvious, the h, g and hI,norm indices for these four academics differ very substantially. However, their hI,annual indices are very similar indeed. Using the hIa might thus be useful to "spot" high performers early in their career.

9 years		20 years		29 years		40 years	
h-index:	24	h-index:	45	h-index:	69	h-index:	82
g-index:	49	g-index:	97	g-index:	167	g-index:	212
hI,norm:	17	hI,norm:	37	hI,norm:	53	hI,norm:	69
hI,annual:	1.89	hI,annual:	1.85	hI,annual:	1.83	hI,annual:	1.73

Obviously, there is no guarantee that the academically younger academics will continue to grow their h-index (and thus hI,norm) during the next 10, 20 or 30 years time. Unless academics keep on publishing high-impact work or their current publications acquire substantially more citations, their hIa will decline naturally with age. Hence, maintaining a high hIa for more than 20 years is indicative of very productive and impactful academics.

PoP tip 42: What the heck are all these metrics (4)? Even more h-indices

There are far more metrics available in Publish or Perish that might interest you if you are a bibliometric researcher or just fascinated by metrics. You can find them by scrolling down in this box.

```
"a harzing": all
Query date: 2015-12-07
Papers: 111
Citations: 9497
Years: 20
```

Advanced metrics for advanced users

The advanced metrics have been hidden from the standard view, as they are irrelevant for most PoP users that tend to be interested in total citations and the h-index only. Formal definitions of all metrics are provided here:

- http://www.harzing.com/pophelp/metrics.htm

That said, there are two additional h-index variants that have attracted considerable attention, the Hc-index and the hI index. Hence I discuss them here.

Hc-index (contemporary h-index)

The Contemporary h-index was proposed by Antonis Sidiropoulos, Dimitrios Katsaros, and Yannis Manolopoulos in their paper **Generalized h-index for disclosing latent facts in citation networks**, *arXiv:cs.DL/0607066 v1 13 Jul 2006*.

It adds an age-related weighting to each cited article, giving (by default; this depends on the parametrization) less weight to older articles. The weighting is parametrized; the Publish or Perish implementation uses gamma=4 and delta=1, like the authors did for their experiments. This means that for an article published during the current year, its citations count four times. For an article published 4 years ago, its citations count only once (4/4). For an article published 6 years ago, its citations count 4/6 times, and so on.

Difference between h-index and hc-index larger for older academics

The difference between the h-index and the hc-index will typically be larger for older academics than for younger academics. However, mid-career academics who have done most of their significant work immediately post-PhD will also have a relatively low hc-index. Going back to our example for the hI,annual, produces the following comparison. For the younger academics the hc-index is fairly similar to their regular h-index, whereas for the older academics it is substantially lower.

Years active	h-index	hc-index	hc/h
9	24	26	1.08
20	45	41	0.91
29	69	53	0.77
40	82	55	0.67

The hc-index even exceeds the h-index for the early career academic, who has done some of his most impactful work in the last 4 years. This also points to a limitation of the h-index: it doesn't work very well if you limit the search to for instance the last 5 years as nearly always becomes higher than the h-index.

hI index (Individual h-index)

The best-known alternative to the hI,norm is the hI index. It was proposed by Pablo D. Batista, Monica G. Campiteli, Osame Kinouchi, and Alexandre S. Martinez (2006) in their paper **Is it possible to compare researchers with different scientific interests?**, *Scientometrics*, 68(1): 179-189.

hI index punishes co-authorship severely

The hI simply divides the h-index by the **average** number of authors in the articles contributing to the h-index. However, this can easily lead to anomalies as the hI-index could be brought down by one modestly cited article with a large number of co-authors. This is true even if most of the academic's citations come from single-authored articles. In general, it includes a very strong "punishment" for co-authorship.

hI, norm favours a more differentiated co-authorship correction

The hI,norm only reduces the number of *citations* for each paper by accounting for the number of co-authors. This means that papers with a large number of citations can still be included in the h-index if their number of citations after co-author correction is high enough. Reviewing our example for the hI,norm, produces the following comparison. As we can see the "punishment" for co-authorship for the hI index is very significant and can completely reverse disciplinary comparisons.

Discipline	h-index	hI,norm	hI,norm/h	hI	hI/h
Social Sciences	45	37	0.82	25.63	0.57
Physics	44	20	0.46	9.05	0.21
Social Sciences	23	20	0.87	9.12	0.46
Humanities	18	18	1.00	18.00	1.00

The Physics Professor's h-index is 2.5 times as high as that of the Humanities Professor. His hI,norm is similar, but his hI is only half of that of the Humanities Professor.

Conclusion: which individual h-index to use?

Someone's preference for this individual h-index over the hI,norm depends on the importance one places on single-authored papers. I would argue that the hI,norm is closest to the initial philosophy of the h-index by focusing on citations, rather than on papers. However, in disciplines where single-authorship is very highly valued, the hI might be a valid alternative.

PoP tip 43: Present your case (1): Find the pearls in your record

The most important realisation in presenting your case for tenure, promotion, or grant applications is to realise that every case is different.

Finding your pearls

We all have "pearls" in our research portfolio. You just need to find and polish them so they shine brightly. Of course sometimes you are prescribed to list a number of metrics, maybe total citation counts, or h-index, or your number of publications. However, even in that case you can always add additional information from Publish or Perish.

Worked example: two different profiles

Remember the comparison between my colleague Maria and myself? We had very similar records in terms of citations per year. However, I would suggest rather different ways of presenting our records to our best advantage.

Ground breaking contributions

As Maria, I would indicate that I had 10 articles that have gathered more than 25 citations per year and that five of my articles have gathered more than 500 citations (see below). I would also point out that I have made a number of ground breaking contributions very early in my career; Maria's six most highly cited articles on a per year basis were all published shortly after her PhD completion.

Cites	Per year	Authors	Title	Year
1586	113.29	SE Seibert, ML Kraimer, RC ...	A social capital theory of career success	2001
1312	93.71	..., RC Liden, SJ Wayne, ML ...	Social networks and the performance of individuals and groups	2001
825	51.56	SE Seibert, JM Crant, ML Kr...	Proactive personality and career success.	1999
685	48.93	SE Seibert, ML Kraimer, JM ...	A longitudinal model linking proactive personality and career success	2001
513	36.64	ML Kraimer, SJ Wayne, RA J...	Sources of support and expatriate performance: The mediating role of ...	2001
465	33.21	SE Seibert, ML Kraimer	The five-factor model of personality and career success	2001
98	32.67	MA Shaffer, ML Kraimer, YP ...	Choices, challenges, and career consequences of global work experien...	2012
123	30.75	ML Kraimer, SE Seibert, SJ ...	Antecedents and outcomes of organizational support for development:...	2011
246	27.33	B Erdogan, RC Liden, ML Kr...	Justice and leader-member exchange: The moderating role of organiza...	2006
282	25.64	B Erdogan, ML Kraimer, RC ...	Work value congruence and intrinsic career success: the compensatory...	2004

However, I would also emphasise that several of my publications in the last five years (publications #7 and #8) also attract high levels of citations. I would probably not discuss co-authorships as this is not a particular strength of Maria's record. One might consider pointing to well-known co-authors, but this is a double-edged sword. To some readers this is a very positive sign, others might wonder about the academic's own contribution.

Sustained and single-authored contributions

As Anne-Wil, I would make a very different case, given that I do not have any articles with extremely high citation levels (i.e. above 500). I would, however, indicate that I have no less than 15 articles that have gathered more than 25 citations per year (see below).

Cites		Per year	Authors	Title	Year
✓	h 436	72.67	NJ Adler, AW Harzing	When knowledge wins: Transcending the sense and nonsense of acade...	2009
✓	h 341	68.20	AW Harzing, A Pinnington	International human resource management	2010
✓	h 474	59.25	AW Harzing	Publish or perish	2007
✓	h 371	46.38	AW Harzing, R Van der Wal	Google Scholar: the democratization of citation analysis	2007
✓	h 472	36.31	AW Harzing	Acquisitions versus greenfield investments: International strategy and ...	2002
✓	h 171	34.20	AW Harzing	The publish or perish book	2010
✓	h 66	33.00	AW Harzing	A preliminary test of Google Scholar as a source for citation data: a lon...	2013
✓	h 196	32.67	N Noorderhaven, AW Harzing	Knowledge-sharing and social interaction within MNEs	2009
✓	h 183	30.50	AW Harzing, R Van Der Wal	A Google Scholar h-index for journals: An alternative metric to measur...	2009
✓	h 263	29.22	AW Harzing	Response Styles in Cross-national Survey Research A 26-country Study	2006
✓	h 435	29.00	AW Harzing	An empirical analysis and extension of the Bartlett and Ghoshal typolog...	2000
✓	h 183	26.14	AW Harzing, AJ Feely	The language barrier and its implications for HQ-subsidiary relationships	2008
✓	h 337	25.92	AW Harzing	Of bears, bumble-bees, and spiders: The role of expatriates in controlli...	2002
✓	h 409	25.56	AW Harzing	Managing the multinationals: An international study of control mechanis...	1999
✓	h 51	25.50	AW Harzing, M Pudelko	Language competencies, policies and practices in multinational corporat...	2013

I would also point out that my most highly cited work is largely first or single-authored and that much of it was published in the second half of my career, thus indicating that my impact has not slowed down after being promoted to Full Professor in 2006. That said; I would probably also emphasise that my PhD thesis (publication #14) and three articles resulting from it (#5, #11, #13) have also quite influential.

Creating effective stories

As I indicated in the introduction of the Publish or Perish book:

> Citations are not only a reflection of the impact that a particular piece of academic work has generated. Citations can also be used to tell stories about academics, journals and fields of research. This book is meant to help you create effective stories.

So go ahead: find the pearls in your record, polish them and string them into a beautifully arranged necklace that presents your citation story.

PoP tip 44: Present your case (2): Create your own reference group

When going up for promotion or tenure, it is usually a good idea to compare your case to a relevant group of peers. Many evaluators have very little idea of what typical norm scores for the various metrics are. So unless you make an explicit comparison, they will explicitly or implicitly use their own reference group, which might not necessarily work to your advantage.

Differences in citation behaviour between disciplines

There are vast differences in typical citation scores between disciplines, especially when using Thomson Reuters Web of Science, i.e. ISI, citation data. Therefore, if your university has a tenure or promotion process in which decisions are made by committees composed of people in related, or even unrelated disciplines, it is even more important to frame your case for tenure or promotion with an appropriate reference group.

Differences in citation behaviour within sub-disciplines

Citation behaviours can also vary dramatically *within* disciplines or even within sub-disciplines. The area of Human Resource Management, as a sub-discipline of Management, includes scholars working on industrial relations and labour unions as well as scholars working on more psychologically oriented topics such as motivation or job attitudes.

HRM: from Organizational Behaviour to Industrial Relations

The latter academics, working in the field of organizational behaviour, might be able to publish in a mainstream Psychology journal such as *Psychological Bulletin.* The former academics would feel most fortunate if they published in the top US journal in their field: *Industrial Relations.* The ISI journal impact factor of *Psychological Bulletin* is about six times as high as the journal impact factor of *Industrial Relations.*

Contextual research is difficult to publish in mainstream US-American journals

Moreover, as their research is very contextual, many Industrial Relations academics will not be able to publish in mainstream US-American Industrial Relations journals. Hence they might need to publish their work in lower impact journals such as *British Journal of Industrial Relations, European Journal of Industrial Relations, Asia Pacific Journal of Human Resources,* or the *Australian Labour History.*

Citations rates in Industrial Relations lower than in Organization Behaviour

Therefore, we can expect any articles in the area of Industrial Relations to be cited far less frequently than articles in the area of Organizational Behaviour, which is more closely related to psychology.

Query	Papers	Cites	Cites/year	h
"Psychological Bulletin" from 2010 to 2015:...	187	22030	4406.00	87
"British Journal of Industrial Relations" fro...	214	2918	583.60	27
"European Journal of Industrial Relations" f...	146	1534	306.80	22
"Labour History", 0023-6942 from 2010 to 2...	196	159	31.80	5

The Publish or Perish screenshot above compares publications in *Psychological Bulletin* from 2010-2015 with a number of Industrial Relations journal and clearly shows how articles in the former can expect much higher citation rates. Looking at how your article compares with other articles in the journal is therefore generally a good strategy.

How to pick your reference group?

It is very important to pick your reference group wisely. Your reference group should be narrow enough to reflect any differences in citation behaviours across disciplines. However, it should not be so narrow that it leads your committee to discard your selection as biased or irrelevant. Generally, I have found two strategies to be particularly effective: the international discipline-based strategy and the institution-based strategy.

A: Discipline strategy: Comparison with academics in the same research field

For the first strategy, you compare your record with a representative selection of academics in your field of research at the level you are applying for. To make your case convincing, it is usually best to pick academics at institutions of similar or higher level of prestige. If you can show you are performing at the same level as academics in more prestigious institutions who have been in position for a while, you have a very strong case.

B: Institutional strategy: Comparison with academics in your own institution

The second strategy is a more local strategy. Here you compare your record with academics in your own institution at the level you are applying for. If you have access to the length of tenure of your academic colleagues, you might be able to compare your record with that of both long-established academics and of those recently promoted to the same level. This strategy might be particularly effective if your institution has more stringent norms for promotion than comparable institutions.

Ensure your reference group is large enough

Please note that you will normally need at least 3-4 academics in your reference group to be able to make a credible comparison and larger numbers are advisable. I would generally advise against listing names of individuals as this can easily lead to a hostile response. However, be prepared to substantiate your averages if so requested. You might wish to create folders for your reference groups in the Publish or Perish multi-query center, so that you can store and update analyses easily.

It is your job to convince the tenure or promotion panel!

In general, please realize that it is your job to convince and educate your tenure or promotion panel of the impact of your research. Many senior academics, having grown up in an age in which citation metrics were relatively unimportant, have a very limited knowledge of their own or other academics' citation records. Moreover, in my experience many academics have the tendency to subconsciously overestimate what their own records were when they went up for tenure or promotion and hence are implicitly using an inappropriate reference group.

"Making your case" is crucial for many processes in academia

If you have an excellent record, you might think it is unfair to have to do all this work to get promoted. You might also think that senior academics should know better, but remember: they are only human and are very busy people. Furthermore, many processes in academia (e.g. further promotions, job applications, grant applications, applications for research awards, and applications for fellowships) depend on you making the case for the impact of your research. Hence it is not a bad idea to get some skills in "selling" your record!

Your notes

PoP tip 45: Present your case (3): Pick your metrics wisely

Publish or Perish provides you with a very wide range of metrics. If your university prescribes the metrics you need to use, you have little choice. However, in many cases there is more flexibility. So what metrics do you pick?

Worked example

The screenshot below shows a summary of my own citation record. Fortunately, my h-index and g-index are relatively high in comparison to other academics in my field, so it is relatively easy for me to make my case.

Results

Papers:	298	Cites/paper:	32.33	h-index:	44	hc-index: 42
Citations:	9635	Cites/author:	7142.16	g-index:	95	hI-index: 25.81
Years:	20	Papers/author:	215.46	hI,norm:	36	hI,norm: 36
						hI,annual: 1.80
Cites/year:	481.75	Authors/paper:	1.77	hI,annual:	1.80	hm-index: 35.92

However, if I had the choice and was applying for a professorial position, I would probably point to the fact that my contemporary h-index and my individual h-index are relatively high in comparison to my regular h-index. I would also point out a relatively high hI,annual. This would allow me to make the case that:

- **Much of my work is recent**. Hence my productivity has not (yet) declined and I am likely to continue making a strong contribution to the field. Academics who have published most of their impactful work long ago will have a low contemporary h-index, even though their regular h-index might be fairly high.

- **My most-cited work is single-authored**. Thus it is easy to substantiate that I have made a significant intellectual contribution. It also shows that my citation record is not inflated by citations from co-authors and their networks. Academics who publish mostly co-authored work will have lower individual h-indices.

- **I have made a sustained contribution**, reflected in my relatively high hI,annual, i.e. on average I have published nearly 2 single-authored equivalent impactful articles every year in the last 20 years.

Early to mid-career academics

Most academics going up for tenure or promotion will benefit from using the contemporary h-index when comparing themselves with current job incumbents, as most of their published work will be relatively recent.

Whether it is beneficial for you to use the individual h-index depends on your number of highly-cited single-authored articles. Publish or Perish provides three implementations of the individual h-index (hI-index, hI,norm and hm-index), so feel free to pick the one that shows of your case to its best advantage!

hI,annual might be particularly useful

The hI,annual can be particularly useful if you are an early or mid-career academic as this metric is often relatively high at this career stage. Using the hIa allows you to compare yourself against more senior academics on an equal footing. Of course, you do need to inspire confidence that you will be able to sustain this level of performance. It is not easy to keep publishing new impactful articles every year!

PoP tip 46: Present your case (4): Compare your best papers to the journal average

In a previous tip, I encouraged you to pick your own reference group. What better reference group than academics who have published in the same journals that you have published in?

Most cited paper in the journal that year

The Publish or Perish screenshot below compares my 2013 paper published in the *Journal of World Business* with other papers published in the same year and finds it is the most highly cited paper in the journal in that particular year.

Journal impact analysis - Perform a citation analysis for one or more journals							

Journal title: "Journal of World Business"

Exclude these words:

Year of publication between: 2013 **and:** 2013

Data source: Google Scholar

Results

Papers:	50	Cites/paper:	15.70	h-index:	16	"Journal of World Business" from 2013 to 2013: all
Citations:	785	Cites/author:	337.18	g-index:	25	Query date: 2015-12-19
Years:	2	Papers/author:	21.55	hI,norm:	11	Papers: 50 Citations: 785
Cites/year:	392.50	Authors/paper:	2.70	hI,annual:	5.50	Years: 2

Cites		Per ...	Authors	Title	Year	Publication
☑ h	51	25.50	AW Harzing, M Pudelko	Language competencies, policies and practices in multinational corporation...	2013	Journal of World Business
☑ h	44	22.00	WT Hsu, HL Chen, CY ...	Internationalization and firm performance of SMEs: The moderating effect...	2013	Journal of World Business
☑ h	40	20.00	M Sarstedt, P Wilczyns...	Measuring reputation in global markets—A comparison of reputation meas...	2013	Journal of World Business
☑ h	38	19.00	J Hessels, SC Parker	Constraints, internationalization and growth: A cross-country analysis of E...	2013	Journal of World Business
☑ h	38	19.00	S Laforet	Organizational innovation outcomes in SMEs: Effects of age, size, and sector	2013	Journal of World business
☑ h	38	19.00	A Klitmøller, J Lauring	When global virtual teams share knowledge: Media richness, cultural differ...	2013	Journal of World Business
☑ h	33	16.50	L Rabbiosi, GD Santan...	Parent company benefits from reverse knowledge transfer: The role of th...	2013	Journal of World Business
☑ h	33	16.50	SG Lee, S Trimi, C Kim	The impact of cultural differences on technology adoption	2013	Journal of World Business
☑ h	29	14.50	Y Fang, M Wade, A De...	An exploration of multinational enterprise knowledge resources and foreig...	2013	Journal of World Business

A comparison like this can be particularly effective as it automatically corrects for differences in citation behaviours across disciplines and differences in papers of a different age. You could write this up in your application as: *"My 2013 paper in Journal of World Business was the most cited paper out of 50 papers published that year and had more than three times as many citations as the average paper in the journal that year."*

Most cited single-authored paper

You can be creative in this as well. The screenshot below shows my 2001 publication in the *Journal of International Business Studies*. Unfortunately, it was not the most cited paper in the journal that year, but it was the 2nd most cited single-authored paper and the 5th most cited paper overall (out of 40), which in a top US journal is a significant achievement.

Journal title: "Journal of International Business Studies"

Exclude these words:

Year of publication between: 2000   and: 2000

Data source: Google Scholar   ▼

Results

Papers:	40	Cites/paper:	200.48	h-index:	36	"Journal of International Business Studies" from 2000 to 2000: all
Citations:	8019	Cites/author:	4409.40	g-index:	40	Query date: 2015-12-19
Years:	15	Papers/author:	22.90	hI,norm:	33	Papers: 40
Cites/year:	534.60	Authors/paper:	2.20	hI,annual:	2.20	Citations: 8019
						Years: 15

Cites		Per ...	Authors	Title	Year	Publication
☑ h	682	45.47	JH Dyer, W Chu	The determinants of trust in supplier-automaker relatio...	2000	Journal of International Business Studies
☑ h	637	42.47	AS Thomas, SL Mueller	A case for comparative entrepreneurship: Assessing th...	2000	Journal of International Business Studies
☑ h	591	39.40	Y Pan, DK Tse	The hierarchical model of market entry modes	2000	Journal of International Business Studies
☑ h	553	36.87	P Ellis	Social ties and foreign market entry	2000	Journal of international business studies
☑ h	436	29.07	AW Harzing	An empirical analysis and extension of the Bartlett and ...	2000	Journal of international business studies

Most cited paper from outside North America

If you work outside North America and have published in a North American journal, you could also make an argument that publishing in these journals tends to be more difficult from outside North America. You could then look at whether your paper is maybe the most cited article by a non-North American academic or the most cited article by an academic from your own country.

Paper in the top-5/top-10 or top 10% most cited

Of course, it will not happen very often that your paper is the most-cited paper in the journal in question. However, even just being able to say that it is within the top-5 or top-10 most cited papers makes a very significant contribution to your case. You can also use percentages – such as "in the top 10% most cited papers in the journal that year" – if this makes your case more impressive.

Most cited paper over longer time period

If you are lucky you have articles that are amongst the most-cited articles in a particular journal over a longer period. If you could say that your article was amongst the top 5% or top 10% most cited articles in a particular journal over its entire history of publication that would make a very strong case, especially if the journal was a particularly well-known journal.

Worked example: top 1% most cited in AMLE

As the screenshot below shows, my article with Nancy Adler in the *Academy of Management Learning & Education* was in the top 1% of articles (5th out of 754) published in AMLE. Given that it was published in 2009, i.e. about mid-way in the journal's lifetime, this might make quite a strong case.

Journal title:	"Academy of Management Learning & Education"
Exclude these words:	
Year of publication between:	and:
Data source:	Google Scholar ▼

Results

Papers:	754	Cites/paper:	43.93	h-index:	84	"Academy of Management Learning & Education": all
Citations:	33123	Cites/author:	21046.21	g-index:	162	Query date: 2015-12-19
Years:	13	Papers/author:	526.55	hI,norm:	66	Papers: 754
						Citations: 33123
Cites/year:	2547.92	Authors/paper:	1.85	hI,annual:	5.08	Years: 13

Cites		Per ...	Authors	Title	Year
☑ h	2682	268.20	S Ghoshal	Bad management theories are destroying good management practices	2005
☑ h	1930	193.00	AY Kolb, DA Kolb	Learning styles and learning spaces: Enhancing experiential learning in higher educ...	2005
☑ h	1483	114.08	J Pfeffer, CT Fong	The end of business schools? Less success than meets the eye	2002
☑ h	467	42.45	B Honig	Entrepreneurship education: Toward a model of contingency-based business planning	2004
☑ h	438	73.00	NJ Adler, AW Harzing	When knowledge wins: Transcending the sense and nonsense of academic rankings	2009

Pay attention to the time period you are reporting on

However, it is not such a good idea to use this strategy if your paper was published early in the time period you are reporting on. For instance, if you claim that your paper is amongst the 25% most cited articles in a journal between 2000-2010, and your paper was published in 2000/2001, it is likely that your paper was actually cited less than average for articles in 2000 and 2001.

Compare a body of work rather than individual papers

If you do not have any papers that really stand out, but your papers are generally well cited in comparison to the journals they are published in, you could emphasize this. For instance, you could say: *on average my articles are amongst the top 20%-30% most cited papers when compared to papers published in the same journal in the same year*. Be careful with this strategy though. Unless you have some papers that have been published in journals that your evaluation committee will recognize as top journals, it will only elicit the comment that you tend to waste your work by publishing in low impact journals.

Your notes

PoP tip 47: Present your case (5): Present comprehensive citation counts for edited volumes

In some disciplines it is very common to publish edited volumes. In these cases the editor typically invests a significant amount of time in coaching contributors to submit their chapters in time, and often provides significant editorial input.

Edited volumes can make a major contribution to the field

Edited volumes can make a major contribution to the field as they typically provide a collection the latest research on a particular topic. Unfortunately, in promotion applications edited volumes are often not appreciated as much as authored books or journal articles.

But their citation impact might be modest

One reason for this might be that the citation impact of these volumes is often quite modest, as few academics will refer to the edited volume as a whole. It is more common for authors to refer to individual chapters within an edited volume.

Worked example

In 1995, I published an edited textbook on International Human Resource Management, with new editions in 2004, 2010/2011 (published in 2010, but copyright of 2011) and 2014. Although it was a textbook, Publish or Perish shows that it generated quite a lot of citations in academic literature. Many of these citations were to the book as a whole, with a combined number of some 350 citations for the various editions.

Journal impact analysis - Perform a citation analysis for one or mo

Journal title:	"International Human Resource Management"
Exclude these words:	
Year of publication between:	1995 and: 1995
Data source:	Google Scholar

Results

| Papers: | 14 | Cites/paper: | 25.64 | h-index: |
| Citations: | 359 | Cites/author: | 276.00 | g-index: |

Journal impact analysis - Perform a citation analysis for one or mo

Journal title:	"International Human Resource Management"
Exclude these words:	
Year of publication between:	2004 and: 2004
Data source:	Google Scholar

Results

| Papers: | 16 | Cites/paper: | 30.50 | h-index: |
| Citations: | 488 | Cites/author: | 403.25 | g-index: |

Journal impact analysis - Perform a citation analysis for one or mo

Journal title: "International Human Resource Management"

Exclude these words:

Year of publication between: 2010   and: 2011

Data source: Google Scholar   ▼

Results

Papers:	7	Cites/paper:	14.86	h-index:	
Citations:	104	Cites/author:	47.47	g-index:	

Comprehensive citation count provides a case for impact

However, as the three screenshots show, there were a further 359 citations to individual chapters in the 1995 edition, 488 to chapters the 2004 edition and 104 to chapters in the 2010/2011 edition. Overall, the book therefore had nearly 1,300 citations (350+359+488+104), a number that would allow me to more easily argue the case that this edited volume has had a significant impact in the field of International Human Resource Management.

PoP tip 48: Present your case (6): Argue for quality by association

If you have only a few citations in either ISI or Google Scholar, it might be worth tracking each of them down to see who is citing your work and in which outlets.

Quality of citations

It is more impressive when many of your citations occur in the top journals in your field or if some famous academics in your field cite your articles. Some of the fame and quality image of the journals and of the academics citing your work might rub off on you in the eyes of your evaluation committee.

Find out who is citing your work

In order to find out who is citing your work, right-click on the work in question and click **Lookup Citations**.

Cites	Per year	Authors	Title	Year
☑ h 452	34.77	AW Harzing	Open Article in Browser	
☑ h 441	73.50	NJ Adler, AW Ha...		
☑ h 436	29.07	AW Harzing	Open Citations/Related in Browser	
☑ h 382	23.88	AW Harzing	Lookup Citations	
☑ h 371	46.38	AW Harzing, R V...		

This opens a new window that allows you to pick a descriptive title for this search. When you click OK, Publish or Perish will retrieve all citing works.

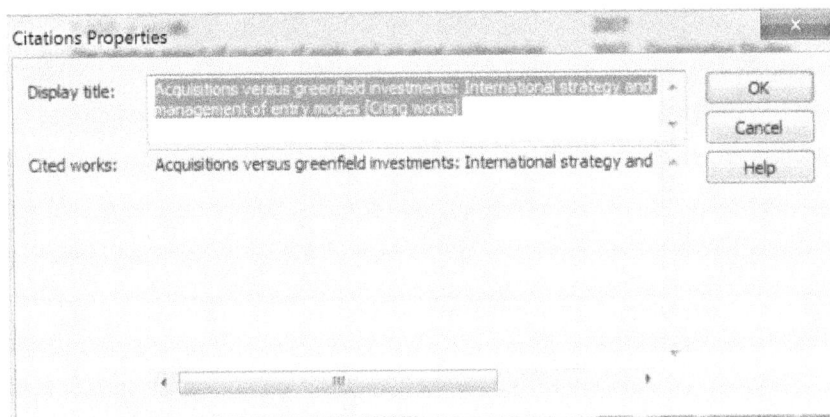

Citations Properties

Display title:	Acquisitions versus greenfield investments: International strategy and management of entry modes [Citing works]	OK
		Cancel
Cited works:	Acquisitions versus greenfield investments: International strategy and	Help

Please use this option sparingly as it does put substantial additional strain on Google Scholar. Whilst it is possible to look up citations for your whole publication list, we do not recommend this if you have more than a few hundred citations. It will take a long time and puts unnecessary strain on Google Scholar.

Quality of outlets

If you have very few citations, you may instead need to focus on the quality of the journals that your work appeared. In general, this is not appropriate, as some papers in top journals never get cited.

Use journal impact factor to argue for future impact

However, on average papers in top journals get cited more than papers in lower-ranked journals. That's why these journals have higher Journal Impact Factors. Therefore, if your work has been published in high-impact journals, you can make the case that it is more likely that your work will be highly cited in the future.

Quality versus impact arguments

In addition, you should of course make the argument that these journals have generally higher quality standards for the work they publish and a more rigorous review process. However, that's a quality argument, not a citation impact argument, and although the two are related, they are not necessarily identical.

PoP tip 49: Evaluating other academics (1): Reviewers, examiners, key note speakers, referees

There is a large variety of possible functions one could think of: reviewers for journals or conferences, examiners for Master of PhD theses, key note speakers, discussants or session chairs for conferences, academic mentors, referees, etc.

In this tip, I will discuss selection as an editorial board member, but the mechanisms involved are very similar for most of these functions. There are several things that an editor/evaluator would be interested in.

Academic credibility

The first question would be: Does the prospective editorial board member (or reviewer or examiner or referee...) have a credible publication record? If one is selecting an editorial board member for a prestigious journal, there should be some evidence of publications that have had an impact on the field and of a sustained stream of research output. This can be easily evaluated looking at the number of publications and citations that PoP reports.

Expertise in the area in question

The prospective editorial board member should also have expertise in the disciplinary orientation of the journal or the sub-discipline that is currently underrepresented. A quick perusal of the titles of his or her publications should be sufficient to establish this.

For some journals it might be important to have a broad orientation so that one is able to review in a range of different, but related areas. Other journals might prefer specialists, either because the journal is a specialist journal itself (e.g. *International Journal of Nuclear Desalination*), or because the journal has a more general orientation, but only publishes the very best research in each sub-discipline (e.g. *Science*).

Experience with the journal

An editor will also want to know whether the prospective editorial board member has experience with the journal. Most journals will keep systematic files on their ad-hoc reviewers. So if the prospective board member has been a successful ad hoc reviewer, they can be expected to have sufficient experience with the journal.

However, editors would normally give preference (or in some cases only consider) academics that have published in the journal themselves. Publish or Perish makes it very easy to run a quick search on this using the General citation search.

Geographical scope

Many journals in the Social Sciences will publish work conducted in different countries. To the extent that the country context matter for the research in question, it is important to have editorial board members with a broad geographical experience.

Although it is not always possible to deduce this from the articles titles, in many cases a quick perusal of the PoP results should provide the editor with a feel for the experience the prospective board members has with research in different countries. Looking at their co-authors might also give some clues, to the extent one can deduce nationality from names.

Caveats

None of these factors can be established with absolute certainty through a simple Publish or Perish search. However, the editor should be able to get a pretty good feel for the prospective board members that are worthy of further investigation.

PoP tip 50: Evaluating other academics (2): Meeting an academic visitor

Do you recognize the following scenario? You are due to meet an official guest of some standing, but you do not know the academic in question very well and hence do not have a clear idea of what he or she is well-known for. You have been running around all day and only have 5-10 minutes before the meeting. How do you ensure you are well prepared and don't blunder your way through the meeting?

Web searches vs PoP searches

You could of course start searching on the web for the academic's university staff page. However, these are not always easy to find, especially if the academic has a relatively common name. Moreover, not all universities allow their staff to create their own web pages and even if they do, they often are out of date as most academics are not very diligent in maintaining them. Publish or Perish offers a quick solution. If you know the academic's given and family name you can use these for a very quick author search, which can allow you to deduce quite a lot in just a couple of minutes.

What are you best known for?

Even though the quick-and-dirty search might not give you fully accurate citation statistics, looking at the most cited works will give you a very quick idea of what the academic in question is best-known for. It might also give you some insight into their publication strategy.

- Do they have a large number of papers that have gathered a reasonable number of citations? That might point to a more diversified publication strategy.
- Do they have one or two papers with a huge number of citations and other less cited work? This might point to a very focused publication strategy.

Who are you working with?

By sorting on the author column, you can quickly find out the academic's co-authors. Maybe you have an academic acquaintance or even collaborator in common? Nothing is better to get a conversation going than talking about people you both know. Looking at an academic's earliest collaborators might also give you a clue about who his/her PhD advisor was. Finding that someone mostly publishes on his/her own is also useful to know. You might not bring up collaborative work in that case, certainly not in a first meeting.

What are you working on recently?

Sorting on the year column helps you finding out what the academic in question has been working on most recently. Most academics don't like it if you talk only about a paper they published ten years ago (even if it is a classic). The research in question might be more than fifteen years old and they might have moved on to completely different topics by now.

How long have you been in the business?

Reviewing the years active statistic gives you some feel for how much academic experience the person you are meeting is likely to have. Of course this might not be of great importance, but again it might change what you will be talking about with this person. Knowing this ahead of time might be helpful. Your conversations with someone in a mid-career stage might be different from those with someone who is close to retirement.

What journals have you published in?

Sorting on the publication column will allow you to find out which journals the academic has published in, giving you an idea of their disciplinary orientation and publication strategy.

- Have they published in general or specialized journals?
- Do they publish mostly conceptual or empirical work?
- Have they published in the top journals in their field?
- Have they published in lots of different journals or focused their output in a small number of journals?

Worked Example: Rabi Bhagat

In July 2010, two of my colleagues had organized a 2-day workshop on Global Teams. One of the keynote speakers was Rabi Bhagat. Although I had seen his name in press before, I could not recall clearly in what context and I had never met him before. I therefore ran a quick Publish or Perish Author Query. The results for his most cited works are below.

Authors	Title	Year
RS Bhagat, BL Kedia, PD Harveston…	Cultural variations in the cross-border transfer of organizational knowledge: An integrat…	2002
K Leung, RS Bhagat, NR Buchan…	Culture and international business: Recent advances and their implications for future re…	2005
BL Kedia, RS Bhagat	Cultural constraints on transfer of technology across nations: Implications for research i…	1988
RS Bhagat, SJ McQuaid	Role of subjective culture in organizations: A review and directions for future research.	1982
SE Sullivan, RS Bhagat	Organizational stress, job satisfaction and job performance: where do we go from here?	1992
RS Bhagat	Effects of stressful life events on individual performance effectiveness and work adjust…	1983
RS Bhagat, SJ McQuaid, H Lindholm…	Total life stress: A multimethod validation of the construct and its effects on organizatio…	1985
TA Beehr, RS Bhagat	Introduction to human stress and cognition in organizations	1985
RS Bhagat, KO Prien	Cross-cultural training in organizational contexts.	1996
RD Arvey, RS Bhagat, E Salas	Cross-cultural and cross-national issues in personnel and human resources management…	1991
TA Beehr, RS Bhagat	Human stress and cognition in organizations: An integrated perspective	1985
AV Phatak, RS Bhagat, RJ Kashlak	International management: Managing in a diverse and dynamic global environment	2005
RS Bhagat, SM Allie, DL Ford	Organizational stress, personal life stress and symptoms of life strains: An inquiry into t…	1991
RS Bhagat, SM Allie	Organizational stress, personal life stress, and symptoms of life strains: An examination…	1989
RS Bhagat, MB Chassie	Determinants of organizational commitment in working women: Some implications for org…	1981
RS Bhagat	Conditions under which stronger job performance–job satisfaction relationships may be …	1982
RS Bhagat, SM Allie, DL Ford	Coping with stressful life events: An empirical analysis	1995

Influential work on culture and knowledge transfer

It was immediately apparent that he had done influential work on the impact of culture on transfer of technology & knowledge across borders. This is most likely where I had seen his name, having done some work on transfer of management practices across cultures myself.

OB/Psychology scholar rather than Strategy scholar

However, I also noticed that he has a fairly large body of work related to stress and stressors in the workplace, stretching from 1985 to 1995. This made me realize that his disciplinary background might be in Organizational Behaviour or even Psychology. His work on technology transfer had led me to the erroneous assumption that he was a macro oriented Strategy scholar.

Working with a varied group of co-authors on mostly conceptual work

The results also showed me that he has worked with a fairly varied group of co-authors, and acted both as first and second author. The titles of his papers led me to conclude that he seems to prefer conceptual work to empirical work as most of his papers are about building theory, creating frameworks and providing an integrative perspective.

Recent work on Asia and global mindsets

Sorting the results by year (see below) showed me that he recently became interested in the role of Asia in management theories and in global mindsets. I also noticed that he has maintained his interest in stress, but has added a cross-cultural element to it.

Authors	Title	Year
MW Peng, RS Bhagat, SJ Chang	Asia and global business	2010
RJ Burke, RS Bhagat, B Krishnan...	Organizational stress, psychological strain, and work outcomes in six national contexts: ...	2010
RS Bhagat, AS McDevitt, I McDevitt	On improving the robustness of Asian management theories: Theoretical anchors in the ...	2010
RS Bhagat, RM Steers	Cambridge handbook of culture, organizations, and work	2009
RS Bhagat, JR Van Scotter, PK Ste...	Cultural variations in individual job performance: Implications for industrial and organiza...	2007
RS Bhagat, HC Triandis, BR Baliga, ...	On becoming a global manager: A closer look at the opportunities and constraints in the...	2007
MH Hoppe, RS Bhagat	Leadership in the United States of America: The leader as cultural hero	2007
RS Bhagat, PK Steverson...	International and Cultural Variations in Employee Assistance Programmes: Implications f...	2007

Recent leadership on multi-country projects

Further, I noticed that although his most cited (older) work is mostly conceptual, his recent articles seem to include empirical work, with data collected in a lot of different countries. Given that he is the first author on these articles, I conclude he was leading those projects. As I have led several multi-country projects myself that might be a nice conversation topic.

Journals published in

Sorting the results by journals showed (amongst others):

- four articles in the *Academy of Management Review* (a journal that only publishes conceptual work),
- three articles each in *Human Relations* (two of which theoretical) and *Journal of Management*, and
- two articles each in *Journal of Organizational Behavior* and *Journal of Vocational Behavior*.

This confirmed my earlier impression that my counterpart was strong in conceptual work. It also confirmed that he was more of a micro Organizational Behaviour scholar than a macro International Business scholar.

In less than 10 minutes, I was ready to meet our keynote speaker. As it turned out, we only talked about Melbourne (the conference location) and Publish or Perish. But at least I felt prepared for any conversation about his academic work!

Conclusion: PoP helps with academic detective work

Even a simple 5-10 minute author search can give you a quick impression of another academic. Obviously, you could do the same type of search in a more rigorous fashion if you were meeting up with someone who could be a potential co-author or if you are lucky enough to have a meeting with your "academic hero". The point is: there is much more to Publish or Perish than finding out someone's h-index or citations. With a bit of detective work you can easily reconstruct a fairly good picture of someone's academic career in a very short space of time.

And finally... find citation connections

Another neat function of Publish or Perish with Google Scholar as the datasource that I only recently discovered myself is to figure out "citation connections" between you and the visitor. Google Scholar searches for keywords in the entire text of full-text document. Hence, a simple General citation search for your own name in the author field and the visitor's name in the any of the words fields will quickly list the articles in which you have cited the visitor's work. Of course this works the other way around as well: you can find out if the visitor has ever cited you. What better way to find out common interests?

PoP tip 51: Evaluating other academics (3): Writing laudations or obituaries

Although these two tasks will generate diametrically opposite emotions, in both cases it is equally important to get a complete overview of someone's impact on the field. It is all too easy to be heavily influenced by a number of contributions that are well known to you personally, whilst forgetting the broader impact that the academic in question might have had.

Worked example: Sumantra Ghoshal

As an example of how to use Publish or Perish in writing obituaries (or review works outlining the impact of a scholar's work) I will focus on Sumantra Ghoshal. His *Managing Across Borders* book with Christopher Bartlett, first published in 1989, was the inspiration for my own PhD work on control mechanisms in multinational companies and I was very shocked to learn of his untimely death at only 55 in 2004.

Cites	Per year	Authors	Title	Year	Publication
h 12556	738.59	J Nahapiet, S Ghoshal	Social capital, intellectual capital, and the organizational advan...	1998	Academy of management review
h 8353	522.06	CA Bartlett, S Ghoshal	Managing across borders: The transnational solution	1999	
h 4663	274.29	W Tsai, S Ghoshal	Social capital and value creation: The role of intrafirm networks	1998	Academy of management Journal
h 2682	268.20	S Ghoshal	Bad management theories are destroying good management pr...	2005	Academy of Management learning & education
h 2485	130.79	S Ghoshal, P Moran	Bad for practice: A critique of the transaction cost theory	1996	Academy of management Review
h 1929	77.16	S Ghoshal, CA Bartlett	The multinational corporation as an interorganizational network	1990	Academy of management review
h 1430	51.07	S Ghoshal	Global strategy: An organizing framework	1987	Strategic management Journal
h 1352	90.13	CA Bartlett, S Ghoshal, J...	Transnational management	2000	
h 931	35.81	S Ghoshal, N Nohria	Internal differentiation within multinational corporations	1989	Strategic management journal
h 927	31.97	S Ghoshal, C Bartlett	Tap your subsidiaries for global reach	1986	Harvard business review
h 850	47.22	N Nohria, S Ghoshal	The differentiated network: Organizing multinational corporatio...	1997	
h 789	29.22	S Ghoshal, CA Bartlett	Creation, adoption, and diffusion of innovations by subsidiaries...	1988	Journal of International Business Studies
h 768	34.91	CA Bartlett, S Ghoshal	Beyond the M-form: Toward a managerial theory of the firm	1993	Strategic Management Journal
h 666	31.71	N Nohria, S Ghoshal	Differentiated fit and shared values: Alternatives for managing...	1994	Strategic Management Journal
h 600	28.57	S Ghoshal, H Korine, G Sz...	Interunit communication in multinational corporations	1994	Management Science
h 598	21.36	CA Bartlett, S Ghoshal	Managing across borders: new strategic requirements	1987	
h 567	22.68	CA Bartlett, S Ghoshal, C...	Managing innovation in the transnational corporation	1990	Managing the global firm
h 559	26.62	S Ghoshal, CA Bartlett	Linking organizational context and managerial action: The dime...	1994	Strategic Management Journal
h 544	54.40	DE Westney, S Ghoshal	Organization theory and the multinational corporation	2005	
h 531	40.85	CA Bartlett, S Ghoshal	Building competitive advantage through people.(Executive Brie...	2002	MIT Sloan Management ...
h 529	24.05	S Ghoshal, N Nohria	Horses for courses: Organizational forms for multinational corp...	1993	Sloan management review

The screenshot above clearly shows that Sumantra Ghoshal's work has had an enormous impact on the field, with more than 20 of his publications generating more than 500 citations and eight of them generating more than 1,000 citations. In total, his work generated more than 55,000 citations, even though less than 20 years had passed between his first publication and his untimely death. However, there are several other conclusions we can derive from the Publish or Perish data.

Combining top scholarship with managerial relevance

The Publish or Perish data clearly illustrate Ghoshal's fairly unique ability to combine rigorous scholarship with work that has managerial relevance.

- He has published a large number of very influential books and has published a large part of his work in more managerially oriented journals such as *Harvard Business Review* and *Sloan Management Review.*
- At the same time, he has published in the top journals in the field of Management and Strategy, such as the *Academy of Management Review/Journal, Strategic Management Journal, Management Science,* and *Journal of International Business Studies.* There are few academics that have combined rigor and relevance so successfully.

There are few academics that have combined rigor and relevance so successfully. Although I was already aware of this before running the search, the Publish or Perish analysis made me realize that even Ghoshal's earliest work, a working paper on scanning behaviour by managers, had a practical slant.

Fighting for a better world

Many academics and students will have been inspired by Ghoshal's last article, published posthumously in the *Academy of Management of Learning & Education*. Entitled "Bad Management Theories are Destroying Good Management Practice", it is a very dramatic analysis of the potential negative impact of academic theories. However, I was unaware that Ghoshal's interest in this field was long-standing with a critique on transaction cost theory published in 1996.

I was also unaware of another posthumous publication "Scholarship that Endures", that appeared in a little-known research annual *Research Methodology in Strategy and Management*, published by Emerald publishers. Even nearly a decade after its publication, there are only four citations to this paper and I can only assume most people are unaware of it. Hence, I am quoting the first paragraph of the article at length, in the hope that it will offer inspiration for current and future scholars:

> "As academics, we collectively publish thousands of articles and hundreds of books each year. We spend a large part of our lives producing them, sacrificing, in the process, sleep, time with our families, reading things we want to read, seeing places we wish to see. Most of these books and articles soon vanish without a trace, helping us get tenure perhaps, but talking with them into oblivion very large parts of the best years of our lives. Few – very few – of the outputs of our intellectual endeavors endure. What is it that distinguishes scholarship that endures from scholarship that does not?" (Ghoshal, 2006: 1)

Serendipitous findings

As an aside, finding Ghoshal's "Scholarship that Endures" article in Google Books also led me to stumble upon another article in the same volume of this research annual that is of substantial relevance to me (Bednar & Westphal, 2006). It deals with improving response rates when surveying corporate elites. It is another article that deserves far more attention than its meagre 2 citations seem to suggest it receives.

Cites		Per year	Authors	Title	Year
☑ h	216	21.60	CL Shook	The dimensionality of organizational performance and its implications for strategic management research	2005
☑ h	68	17.00	A Langley, C Abdallah	Templates and turns in qualitative studies of strategy and management	2011
☑ h	129	14.33	NP Podsakoff, W Shen...	The role of formative measurement models in strategic management research: review, critique, and imp...	2006
☑ h	117	10.64	MA Hitt, BK Boyd, D Li	The state of strategic management research and a vision of the future	2004
☑ h	98	9.80	JB Barney, TB Mackey	Testing resource-based theory	2005
☑ h	43	7.17	M Ganco, G Hoetker	NK modeling methodology in the strategy literature: bounded search on a rugged landscape	2009
☑ h	34	5.67	HG Ridder, C Hoon, A McC...	The theoretical contribution of case study research to the field of strategy and management	2009
☑ h	54	4.91	PS Barr	Current and potential importance of qualitative methods in strategy research	2004
☑ h	48	4.80	RD Ireland, JW Webb, JE ...	Theory and methodology in entrepreneurship research	2005
☑ h	50	4.55	SF Slater, K Atuahene-Gima	Conducting survey research in strategic management	2004
☑ h	36	4.50	JM Shaver	Interpreting empirical results in strategy and management research	2007

I therefore ran a search for articles published in this research annual (screenshot above) and discovered a large number of highly intriguing titles, often written by well-known scholars. However, most of these articles seem to have generated little interest so far, with only a few drawing more than 10 citations per year. It is exactly these kinds of serendipitous findings that are facilitated by Publish or Perish and Google Scholar.

PoP tip 52: Evaluating other academics (4): Publication awards

Citation impact is one factor for publication awards

Many journals give out some type of best paper award on a yearly basis. One of the factors that are often considered when awarding best journal article prizes is the (citation) impact a particular article has had. This is relatively easy to do when the awards are given 10 years after publications, as is for instance the case with the *Journal of International Business Studies* decade award.

Citation impact within 1-2 years is typically modest

However, most journal article prizes are awarded 1 or 2 years after the articles are published. Especially in the Social Sciences and Humanities there are few articles that gather significant citation impact in such a short time.

Worked example: AMLE outstanding article of the year award

In 2010, my article with Nancy Adler (*When Knowledge Wins: the Sense and Nonsense of Academic Ranking*) won the 2009 outstanding article of the year for the *Academy of Management Learning and Education* journal in which it was published. I hope this was mainly because of the article's content, which cautioned against an exclusive focus on academic rankings and discussed the importance of doing research that has relevance to societal problems. However, it is likely that the decision was at least partially influenced by the article's citation impact.

Virtually no ISI citations for AMLE at the time of award decision

Unfortunately, around April 2010, when the award decision was taken, the ISI Web of Science had only incorporated articles from the first (March) issue of the *Academy of Management Learning & Education*, with the three remaining 2009 issues still in process. Of these March articles there was one article with 18 citations (the awarded paper), two articles with 4 citations and several articles with 1-3 citations for a total of 38 citations for AMLE for 2009. Hence, ISI data would have been pretty useless in assessing the impact of articles published in AMLE in 2009.

Google Scholar provides comprehensive citation data

Looking at Google Scholar data in Publish or Perish (see screenshot), the picture is entirely different. All 2009 AMLE papers are included. Although the awarded article is still the most cited article in the journal, there are fourteen (not two) other articles with at least 4 citations and the total number of citations to AMLE articles published in 2009 is 179, not 38. From this, I would conclude that many articles published in this journal do have a fairly substantial immediate impact.

Papers:	55	Cites/paper:	3.25	h-index:	6	AWCR:	89.50
Citations:	179	Cites/author:	105.51	g-index:	11	AW-index:	9.46
Years:	2	Papers/author:	35.75	hc-index:	10	AWCRpA:	52.76
Cites/year:	89.50	Authors/paper:	1.98	hI-index:	3.27	e-index:	7.62
				hI,norm:	6	hm-index:	5.83

Cites		Authors	Title
✓ 🗋	56	NJ Adler, AW Harzing	When knowledge wins: Transcending the sense and nonsense of academic rankings
✓	10	SS Taylor, D Ladkin	Understanding arts-based methods in managerial development
✓	8	MP Bell, ML Connerle...	The case for mandatory diversity education
✓	7	MF Özbilgin	From journal rankings to making sense of the world
✓	7	RS Rubin, EC Dierdorff	How relevant is the MBA? Assessing the alignment of required curricula and required
✓	6	RA Giacalone	Academic rankings in research institutions: A case of skewed mind-sets and professi
✓	6	DL Worrell	Assessing Business Scholarship: The Difficulties in Moving Beyond the Rigor—Releva
✓	6	D Lindebaum	Rhetoric or remedy? A critique on developing emotional intelligence
✓	6	SM Nkomo	The seductive power of academic journal rankings: Challenges of searching for the
✓	5	SH Barr, T Baker, SK...	Bridging the Valley of Death: Lessons Learned From 14 Years of Commercialization o
✓	4	M Blasco	Cultural pragmatists? Student perspectives on learning culture at a business school
✓	4	I Metz, AW Harzing	Gender diversity in editorial boards of management journals
✓	4	MP Bell	Introduction: special section, doing work that matters
✓	4	PH Phan, DS Siegel, ...	New developments in technology management education: background issues, progr

Use Google Scholar data as early indicator of impact

However, even in cases where ISI **does** have complete data for the journal in question, I would recommend using Google Scholar data instead when evaluating papers for publication awards. Google Scholar citations are a much better indicator of early impact as they include citations in conference papers and working papers, most of which will eventually find their way to published articles.

PoP tip 53: Evaluating other academics (5): Preparing for a job interview

We have all been there: you are invited for a job interview and you want to be well-prepared. As part of your search you want to find out what academics in the university you applied for are working on. You might even want to do this **before** applying for the job to decide whether this is the place for you, or simply to tailor your application.

It is all about creating a connection

Remember: most shortlisted applicants for the job are well qualified and will do a good job in their research presentation and teaching demonstration. What matters most is that you create a connection with the people on your interview or shortlist panel. They should be able to picture you as a person they **could**, and would **want to**, work with.

Being well prepared helps building connections

As far as I know, personal chemistry is impossible to engineer. However, there is a lot you can do to increase the chances of building a connection by being well prepared. There are several ways you could approach this, discussed in more detail below. Please note that I am not suggesting you should misrepresent your academic record or compromise your own personal values. However, you can easily emphasize different aspects of your academic record depending on who is on your panel.

Find out what your panel members are working on

Publish or Perish gives you a quick and easy way to find out what the academics on your interview panel are best known for. Simply do an "author impact search" for each of the members of your interview panel. You might also want to read some of these articles in order to be able to make intelligent comments about them.

- ### Find out about their recent research interests

It would also be a good idea to find out what the **recent** research interests of the members on your panel are by sorting their publications by year. You might find out that some of them have similar interests or are even working on papers together. This is something you could comment positively on in your interview, while indicating that working with colleagues is something you aspire to in your job.

- ### Spot synergies in their work

This strategy is even more effective if the panel members didn't know they were working on similar topics. Never underestimate how little many academics know about their colleagues! Although comments on this might work out negatively in some institutions, in most cases the panel will be impressed if you have spotted synergies they were not aware of.

Find out where your panel members are publishing

When searching for your panel members' publications, also make sure you sort the results by publication. This allows you to find out whether there are any journals they have published in regularly.

- ### Create a connection through journals

Many academics have their favourite journals and they will tend to think positively about applicants targeting the same journals. This might be because targeting the same journals automatically reflects a similarity in academic norms and values, or simply because your panel members are more aware of the (high) quality standards of the journals they are personally familiar with.

- ### Which of your projects should you focus on?

I am not proposing you should lie about where you are targeting your work. However, doing a quick search to find out which journals your panel members tend to publish in heavily, might give you some clues about which of your research projects to focus on. It might also lead you to emphasize in your job interview that you have been doing ad-hoc reviewing for this particular journal (only if this is true of course).

- ### Type of publications shows what institution values

Reviewing the **type** of outlets that panel members publish in also gives you an idea of what is valued in the institution you are applying to. Are they mainly publishing in top US academic journals, are they publishing in wider variety of journals, do professional journals feature as an outlet, have any of them written books? None of these publication strategies are inherently superior to others, but it is useful to be aware what seems to be valued most by the institution in question.

- ### Use your research to prepare questions

You could use this as a lead-in to a question of what would be expected of you in terms of publication output if you joined the institution. Most interviews panels **really** appreciate it if you ask questions pro-actively rather than just answer theirs. However, what they appreciate most are **informed** questions.

Find out who are citing your panel members work

In order to **really** impress, you could try to read some of the articles that have built on the panel members' important works and comment intelligently on how they have done this. Many academics are not really aware who is citing their work, so that knowledge might make an excellent impression.

- ### Find a paper that you can talk comfortably about

You can find these citing articles easily. Simply right-click on the paper in question; in the pop-up menu, click on **Lookup Citations**. Pick one that is related to a topic you know a lot (or at least something) about, so that you can talk comfortably about it. This might be an easy way to give you a connection to a person in the panel.

- Find a paper by an academic you know well

Alternatively, pick an article written by an academic you know very well. If you are lucky your panel member knows the academic too, but didn't know that he or she cited their work. There is nothing like common acquaintances to build a quick connection!

- A strategy even more useful to impress a Dean

I can particularly recommend this strategy when some of your panel members are senior administrators such as Deans or Department Chairs. Oftentimes their heavy administrative load has prevented these academics from publishing much in recent years. They will be very pleased to be reminded that their research is still cited!

Find out more about the university

Most junior applicants are too narrowly focused on the job in question and their future department or school. Showing you know more about the university as a whole indicates you have made a real effort. It also signals that you are potential leadership material as you are able to take a broader perspective.

- Find out what the university is well-known for

Find out what is the university well known for. You can search for the University's most cited publications using a general search. Make sure though that to double-check that the university in question is listed as an affiliation of the author, not in the references or any other part of the publication.

- Spot synergies across the university

Having found out what your panel members are working on, try to establish whether there is anyone else in the university working on similar topics. You can do this in the general search function by including the topic and the university in question. Your interview panel will be impressed if you have identified another academic in their university that shares their research interests, especially if they weren't even aware of him/her.

- Link this to multi-disciplinarity

You could even try to link this to a more general discussion on multi-disciplinarity and your own views on this. Although some universities might equate multidisciplinary research with a lack of depth, many universities acknowledge these days that big world problems can only be solved with multidisciplinary research.

Your notes

PoP tip 54: Tips for Deans and other administrators

Publish or Perish tends to be used mostly by individual academics that have full knowledge of their own publication records. However, it is unavoidable that it will also be used by university administrators who might be short of time and short of knowledge about bibliometrics. So what advice can I give to administrators who want to maintain rigorous standards, but also want to be fair and equitable?

Give up your reservations about Google Scholar

First, especially if you work in the Social Sciences and Humanities, or in Engineering and Computer Science, give up your reservations about Google Scholar. These days, many universities allow or even recommend the use of Google Scholar and Publish or Perish. Institutions such World Bank and Microsoft's research laboratory use it to evaluate their broader impact beyond ISI listed journals. Many US government departments use it to evaluate the impact of particular research projects. You can always ask applicants to provide ISI or Scopus data as well, but do take Google Scholar data seriously.

Yes, some of Google Scholar's results are nonsensical. Yes, occasionally Google Scholar will double-count citations. Yes, some of the citations are not as scholarly as one would want. However, these minor errors are not worth worrying too much about when comparing them with the **systematic** and **very large** underestimation of citations in ISI or even Scopus for many disciplines.

Give up your fixation with self-citations

Second, give up your fixation with self-citations. Yes, occasionally academics abuse the system and systematically cite their own work. However, there are safeguards against this system as journal editors and reviewers will not like gratuitous citations. Moreover, if academics are so unethical, they probably have bigger problems than their inflated citation record. For the majority of academics self-citations do not distort their citation records in any significant way. The hassle and possible inconsistency in excluding self-citations is not worth the small possible gain in accuracy.

Be very hesitant in applying citation analysis for junior academics

Third, be very hesitant in applying citation analysis for junior academics, especially in the Social Sciences and Humanities. It can easily take 5-10 years after an academic's first publication before a significant number of citations flows in. Hence, if an early career academic shows a large number of citations, make sure you promote them and keep them happy (assuming other aspects of their performance are also at least satisfactory). However, if academics going up for tenure have very few citations, don't hold it against them.

Realize that citations can vary dramatically between and within disciplines

Fourth, realize that citations can vary dramatically between or even within disciplines. Never compare citation (or publication) records across disciplines. If for some reason you have to do so, use Google Scholar, not ISI or Scopus and preferably use a discipline corrected metric, such as the hI,annual (see reference).

Be very hesitant to prescribe norm scores for the number of citations to be accumulated before someone is considered for tenure or promotion to a certain level. If you feel you do need to prescribe norm scores, make sure they are realistic and reflect actual performance of those at similar levels. Too many senior academics seriously overestimate the number of citations they had themselves when being promoted.

Consult an expert

Fifth, if you have any doubts about what you are doing, consult an expert. Academics and administrators at this level are far too busy to try to understand the minutia of citation analysis. Get a proper bibliometric expert involved! You might have access to a librarian with good skills in this respect or you might have academics in your staff who do bibliometric research. If you do not, read the rest of this course as well. If you read it closely, you'll probably know more about citation analysis than 99.9% of the academics.

References

- Harzing, A.W.; Alakangas, S.; Adams, D. (2014) **hIa: An individual annual h-index to accommodate disciplinary and career length differences**, *Scientometrics*, vol. 99, no. 3, pp. 811-821.

PoP tip 55: Where to submit your paper? (1): Examine which journals publish on your topic

Let's assume you have written a paper, but are unsure which journal to submit it to. Normally, you would already have a pretty good idea of suitable journals through your literature review, but there might be good reasons why you haven't been able to settle on a journal yet.

- You might want to ensure you haven't neglected any options.
- You might know what the most suitable journal would be, but you have already published several papers there and are keen to show the impact of your work beyond your immediate academic peer group.
- The most appropriate journal is one with which you have recently had a bad experience in the review process (e.g. long delays or shoddy reviewer reports).

Use General citation search to search for keywords

What you can do in this case is use the **General citation search** option in Publish or Perish and conduct search a search with the most important key-words in your paper. If you search for a relatively generic topic, many of the hits you get will be books, especially in the Social Sciences and Humanities. Books tend to be highly cited, because they contain more citable material than short journal articles. This is especially true for classic works in the field.

Sort the results by publication outlet

As we are not intending to write a book, the best way to find appropriate journals is to sort the results by publication outlet by clicking on the Publication column. As the default sort for Publish or Perish is the number of citations, clicking on the Publication column will result in a list that is sorted by publication outlet first and then by the number of citations. Scrolling down the list easily allows one to identify the journals that contain articles on your topic and also shows us which of these are most highly cited.

Worked example: Ethical marketing

Let's assume you have written a paper about ethical marketing. You have already noticed that the top-ranked mainstream marketing journals such as *Journal of Marketing* and *Journal of Consumer Research* do not seem to publish a lot of papers on this topic and hence are looking for alternative options.

Use either "The phrase" or "All of the words" field

You would enter the words *ethical marketing* in the **The phrase** box. This will provide any articles in which the words *ethical marketing* appear in that particular order. You will get the same results by including the search term *ethical marketing* in quotes ("*ethical marketing*") in the **All the words** field. If you include the search term *ethical marketing* without quotes it provides many more matches as it matches the words in any order. There will be lots of publications that include both these relatively generic words.

As you want to ensure that the journal has published on ethical marketing in recent years, you limit the search to the last decade (this particular search was conducted in 2010, so results found range between 2000 and 2010).

The result: a neat list of popular journal outlets

The search resulted in 874 hits (including duplicates). As expected many of the most-cited works were books, often fairly generic ones on Marketing Research, Consumer Behaviour and International Marketing. However, sorting the results by publication allows us to identify the most important journal outlets. Below, you will find screenshots with the most frequently occurring journals in this search, with a brief discussion of the results for each.

Journal of Business Ethics

The *Journal of Business Ethics* is the most frequently mentioned journal in our search. The screenshot below shows some of the most cited papers. Although there are a number of papers relating to marketing, most of the papers seem to deal mostly with general business ethics. Even so, this could be an option for Marketing academics who want to reach out to a more general audience interested in ethics.

Title	Year	Publication
A review of empirical studies assessing ethical decision making in business	2000	Journal of Business Ethics
A cross cultural comparison of the contents of codes of ethics: USA, Canada and …	2000	Journal of Business Ethics
Unpacking the ethical product	2001	Journal of Business Ethics
A partnership model of corporate ethics	2002	Journal of Business Ethics
Cross-cultural methodological issues in ethical research	2000	Journal of Business Ethics
An empirical investigation of the relationships between ethical beliefs, ethical ideo…	2001	Journal of Business Ethics
Ethics in personal selling and sales management: a review of the literature focusi…	2000	Journal of Business Ethics
An ethical exploration of privacy and radio frequency identification	2005	Journal of Business Ethics
Ethics and Marketing on this Internet: Practitioners' Perceptions of Societal, Indu…	2000	Journal of Business Ethics
The questionable use of moral development theory in studies of business ethics: …	2001	Journal of Business Ethics
Packaging ethics: Perceptual differences among packaging professionals, brand …	2000	Journal of Business Ethics
International marketing ethics from an Islamic perspective: a value-maximization …	2001	Journal of Business Ethics
Gender differences in ethical perceptions of salespeople: An empirical examinatio…	2002	Journal of Business Ethics
Ethical judgment and whistleblowing intention: examining the moderating role of l…	2003	Journal of Business Ethics
Is cross-cultural similarity an indicator of similar marketing ethics?	2001	Journal of Business Ethics

Journal of Macromarketing

The second most frequently listed journal in our search is *Journal of Macromarketing*. The screenshot below shows all of the hits in order of the number of citations. The first article in the list is the most frequently cited journal article in the entire search. Unfortunately, this is partly caused by a Google Scholar fluke that attributed the citations to the original 1986 article to the 2006 update, similar to aggregating citations to new editions of a book. Even so, it is still the most cited article on the topic if we relax the "last ten years" restriction.

Title	Year	Publication
The general theory of marketing ethics: a revision and three questions	2006	Journal of macromarketing
Normative perspectives for ethical and socially responsible marketing	2006	Journal of Macromarketing
Building understanding of the domain of consumer vulnerability	2005	Journal of Macromarketing
Quality-of-life (QOL) marketing: Proposed antecedents and consequences	2004	Journal of Macromarketing
Macro measures of consumer well-being (CWB): a critical analysis and a researc...	2006	Journal of Macromarketing
Globalization and technological achievement: Implications for macromarketing an...	2004	Journal of Macromarketing
Research on marketing ethics: A systematic review of the literature	2007	Journal of Macromarketing
Distributive justice: Pressing questions, emerging directions, and the promise of ...	2008	Journal of Macromarketing
Research on consumer well-being (CWB): Overview of the field and introduction...	2007	Journal of Macromarketing
The small and long view	2006	Journal of Macromarketing
Voluntary codes of ethical conduct: Group membership salience and globally inte...	2007	Journal of Macromarketing
On Economic Growth, Marketing Systems, and the Quality of Life	2009	Journal of Macromarketing
Assessing distributive justice in marketing: a benefit-cost approach	2007	Journal of Macromarketing
Globalization, transformation, and quality of life: Reflections on ICMD-8 and par...	2004	Journal of Macromarketing
Limited choice: An exploratory study into issue items and soldier subjective well-...	2006	Journal of Macromarketing
Handbook of Quality-of-Life Research: An Ethical Marketing Perspective, by M. ...	2003	Journal of Macromarketing
Applying Catholic Social Teachings to Ethical Issues in Marketing	2009	Journal of Macromarketing
Medicalization and Marketing	2010	Journal of Macromarketing

The journal has also published a range of other highly cited papers in this field and as such might be an appropriate outlet. However, much of the published research seems to focus on high-level societal issues, quality of life or consumer well-being. This is also reflected in its editorial statement: *"The Journal of Macromarketing examines important social issues, how they are affected by marketing, and how society influences the conduct of marketing."* Whether or not this suits your paper obviously depends on its topic.

European Journal of Marketing

The journal with the third largest number of hits to the search for keywords ethical marketing was the *European Journal of Marketing*. The screenshot below shows all resulting papers in order of number of citations. Unfortunately, Google Scholar sometimes abbreviates the title of a journal (see the first five hits, see also Google Scholar: Truncation). This means that the citation order is not perfect as it starts again with the first article for the non-abbreviated journal title, i.e. the *"Grounded theory..."* article has more citations than most of the preceding articles. However, as we are mainly interested in journal outlets at the moment, this is not a serious problem.

Title	Year	Publication
How important are ethics and social responsibility?	2001	European Journal of ...
Moral philosophies of marketing managers	2002	European Journal of ...
An ethical basis for relationship marketing: a virtue ethics perspective	2007	European journal of ...
Corporate social responsibility: investigating theory and research in the marke...	2008	European Journal of ...
Children's impact on innovation decision making	2009	European Journal of ...
Grounded theory, ethnography and phenomenology	2005	European journal of Marketing
Societal marketing and morality	2002	European Journal of Marketing
Marketing as a profession: on closing stakeholder gaps	2002	European Journal of Marketing
Futures dilemmas for marketers: can stakeholder analysis add value?	2005	European Journal of Marketing
Ethics and value creation in business research: comparing two approaches	2006	European Journal of Marketing
An ethical basis for relationship marketing: a virtue ethics perspective The Aut...	2007	European Journal of Marketing

Perusing the titles, it is clear that the *European Journal of Marketing* has a rather broad focus, publishing papers in a variety of areas in marketing. This is reflected in its mission statement: *"We welcome novel and ground-breaking contributions from a wide range of research traditions within the broad domain of marketing"*. This statement also mentions: *"The EJM is receptive to controversial topics, and new, as well as developments that challenge existing theories and paradigms."* Hence, at first glance, this might not be a bad outlet for a topic that is not yet part of the mainstream in Marketing.

Journal of Consumer Marketing

As shown in the screenshot below, the *Journal of Consumer Marketing* has also published a substantial number of papers containing the key words ethical marketing in the past decade. Not surprisingly, most of these papers focus on the ethical consumer. Hence this journal would be a very appropriate outlet if your paper focused on the ethical aspects of consumer behaviour.

Title	Year	Publication
Shopping for a better world? An interpretive study of the potential for ethical...	2004	Journal of Consumer ...
"To legislate or not to legislate": a comparative exploratory study of privacy...	2003	Journal of consumer ...
An inquiry into the ethical perceptions of sub-cultural groups in the US: Hispa...	2002	Journal of Consumer ...
Consumers' Rules of Engagement in Online Information Exchanges	2009	Journal of Consumer ...
The myth of the ethical consumer -do ethics matter in purchase behaviour?	2001	Journal of consumer marketing
The ethicality of altruistic corporate social responsibility	2002	Journal of Consumer Marketing
Consumer privacy and the Internet in Europe: a view from Germany	2003	Journal of Consumer Marketing
Neuromarketing: a layman's look at neuroscience and its potential application...	2007	Journal of Consumer Marketing

Journal of Public Policy & Marketing

Another article with a fairly large number of papers on this topic is *Journal of Public Policy & Marketing*. Perusing the article titles, its topics appear to have some overlap with the *Journal of Macromarketing*. This is confirmed when we look at its editorial statement: *Journal of Public Policy & Marketing has adopted the noteworthy mission of publishing thoughtful articles on how marketing practice shapes and is shaped by societally important factors such as ...* Hence it appears as if these two journals would be particularly appropriate if your paper focused on the societal issues surrounding ethical marketing.

Title	Year	Publication
Does Fair Trade deliver on its core value proposition? Effects on income, e...	2009	Journal of Public Policy & ...
The philosophy and methods of deliberative democracy: Implications for p...	2009	Journal of Public Policy & ...
Marketing to the Poor: An Integrative Justice Model for Engaging Impoveri...	2009	Journal of Public Policy & ...
Consumer online privacy: legal and ethical issues	2000	Journal of Public Policy & Marketing
Antiglobal challenges to marketing in developing countries: Exploring the id...	2005	Journal of Public Policy & Marketing
Ethics and Public Policy Implications of Research on Consumer Well-Being	2008	Journal of Public Policy & Marketing
Principle-Based Stakeholder Marketing: Insights from Private Triple-Bottom...	2010	Journal of Public Policy & Marketing
Ethical Beliefs and Information Asymmetries in Supplier Relationships	2010	Journal of Public Policy & Marketing

Journal of Marketing education

A rather surprising discovery was the fact that the *Journal of Marketing Education* had published a fairly large number of papers in this area. Hence if your paper had any links to marketing education or investigated perceptions of marketing students, this might be an appropriate outlet for your article.

Title	Year	Publication
The effects of marketing education and individual cultural values on marketing...	2002	Journal of Marketing Education
Important factors underlying ethical intentions of students: Implications for m...	2004	Journal of Marketing Education
The Impact of Corporate Culture, the Reward System, and Perceived Moral I...	2005	Journal of Marketing Education
Teaching marketing law: A business law perspective on integrating marketing ...	2000	Journal of Marketing Education
Designing discussion activities to achieve desired learning outcomes: Choices ...	2007	Journal of Marketing Education
Group-Based Assessment as a Dynamic Approach to Marketing Education	2009	Journal of Marketing Education

Journal of the Academy of Marketing science

In your literature review you had already discovered that the mainstream marketing journals do not tend to publish much in the area of ethical marketing. It should therefore come as a pleasant surprise to see that *Journal of the Academy of Marketing Science*, one of the top general marketing journals has published four articles on the broad topic in the past decade.

Title	Year	Publication
Representing the perceived ethical work climate among marketing employ...	2000	Journal of the Academy of ...
Consumer online privacy concerns and responses: a power–responsibility...	2007	Journal of the Academy of Marketing
Marketing with integrity: ethics and the service-dominant logic for marketing	2008	Journal of the Academy of Marketing.
A simulation of moral behavior within marketing exchange relationships	2007	Journal of the Academy of Marketing.

Concomitant with its general marketing status, its editorial statement indicates that articles in a very broad range of topics are acceptable, including ethics and social responsibility. Hence, if you feel your article is of sufficient quality to merit publication in one of the top journals in marketing, this might be an appropriate choice to reach the widest possible audience in the broad field of marketing.

Using the "title words only" box to further refine results

Judging from the titles in the results above, some articles didn't really seem to have a major focus on ethical marketing, but instead simply mentioned the words somewhere in the article. Another option therefore is to narrow down your results by clicking the **Title words only** box. The results will only contain articles that have the words ethical marketing (in that order) in their title, although the words do not necessarily appear close together. The screenshot below produces the results in order of the number of citations.

Comparing the journal titles with our previous results shows that most of the same journals appear in the list. However, there are five new journals that appear on the scene: *Journal of Business Research*, the *Academy of Marketing Science Review*, *Journal of Consumer Affairs*, *Ethics & Behavior* and *Journal of International Marketing*. These journals did not feature on our list before as they only published one or two papers on ethical marketing. However, if the titles appear relevant to your paper, they might be worth considering.

Title	Year	Publication
Normative perspectives for ethical and socially responsible marketing	2006	Journal of Macromarketing
Representing the perceived ethical work climate among marketing employees	2000	Journal of the Academy of …
Important factors underlying ethical intentions of students: Implications for ma…	2004	Journal of Marketing Education
Perceived risk, moral philosophy and marketing ethics: mediating influences on …	2002	Journal of Business research
Ethical guidelines for marketing practice: A reply to Gaski & some observations …	2001	Journal of Business Ethics
Consumer interests and the ethical implications of marketing: a contingency fra…	2003	Journal of Consumer Affairs
Ethical marketing for competitive advantage on the internet	2001	Academy of Marketing Science
The Impact of Corporate Culture, the Reward System, and Perceived Moral In…	2005	Journal of Marketing Education
An ethical basis for relationship marketing: a virtue ethics perspective	2007	European journal of …
Ethical trends in marketing and psychological research	2001	Ethics & Behavior
Sustainable Tourism: Ethical Alternative or Marketing Ploy?	2007	Journal of business ethics
The impact of cultural values on marketing ethical norms: A study in India and t…	2006	Journal of International …

PoP tip 56: Where to submit your paper? (2): Comparing journals by impact

After creating a "short-list" of journals that you might want to publish your paper in, one of the criteria to make your final choice might be the standing or rank of the journal.

Journal rankings: stated vs. revealed preference

In general we can distinguish two broad approaches to ranking journals: stated preference (or peer review) and revealed preference (Tahai & Meyer, 1999). Stated preference involves members of particular academic community ranking journals on the basis of their own expert judgments.

Hundreds of stated preference rankings

There are hundreds of individual university journal rankings. Harzing's Journal Quality List (JQL) aggregates a range of these rankings in Economics & Business. Opinions might be based on anything from a large-scale worldwide survey of academics to a small group of individuals with decision-making power, but will always contain some element of subjectivity.

Revealed preference: ISI's Journal Impact Factor

Revealed preference rankings are based on *actual* publication behaviour and generally measure the citation rates of journals using Thomson ISI's Web of Knowledge. Most commonly used is the ISI Journal Citation Reports (JCR), which provide the yearly Journal Impact Factors (JIF). However, any source of citation data can be used. Publish or Perish is ideally suited to measure the impact of journals with Google Scholar data.

Strong correlation between stated and revealed preference

Mingers and Harzing (2007) show that there is a high degree of correlation between journal rankings based on stated and revealed preference. However, as Tahai & Meyer (1999) point out, stated preference studies have long memories: perceptions of journals normally change only slowly. As such, revealed preference studies provide a fairer assessment of new journals or journals that have recently improved their standing. Therefore, revealed preference studies can present a more accurate picture of journal impact.

Worked example: Accounting journals

Because of differences in accounting rules across countries, Accounting is a localized discipline. As a result, not many of its journals are listed in the Thomson's Journal Citation Reports. Only 30% of the journals in Finance & Accounting listed on the JQL are included in ISI. In contrast, three quarters or more of the journals listed on the JQL in Economics or Management Information Systems are ISI listed. Hence, if one wants to compare the citation impact of Accounting journals, using Google Scholar and Publish or Perish is often the only alternative.

The table below lists a selection of Accounting journals, including the journals generally recognized as the top-5 accounting journals. The table first lists the ISI Journal Impact Factor for 2009 (where available) and the ABDC (Australian Business Dean's Council) rank, a popular journal ranking list in Australia.

Journal Name	ISI JIF 2009	ABDC ranking	GS cites pp	GS h-index	GS g-index
Jnl of Accounting Research	2.350	A*	24.20	43	74
Review of Accounting Studies	1.500	A*	23.64	28	51
Contemporary Accounting Research	1.087	A*	16.87	28	45
Accounting, Organizations and Society	1.803	A*	15.28	34	49
Accounting Review (The)	1.920	A*	15.20	37	56
European Accounting Review	0.633	A	10.88	23	37
Accounting and Business Research	Not listed	A	9.62	15	25
Jnl of Accounting and Public Policy	Not listed	A	9.23	19	30
Accounting Horizons	Not listed	A	8.45	17	27
Accounting, Auditing & Accountability Jnl	Not listed	A	7.63	22	31
Int Jnl of Accounting Inf Systems	Not listed	A	7.20	16	21
British Accounting Review	Not listed	A	6.85	15	22
International Jnl of Accounting	Not listed	A	6.63	15	21
Critical Perspectives on Accounting	Not listed	A	5.42	20	29
Behavioral Research in Accounting	Not listed	A	4.78	9	14
Issues in Accounting Education	Not listed	A	3.20	11	17

PoP impact analysis for 2005-2010

It then reports on the results of a Publish or Perish impact analysis for papers published in the journals between 2005 and July 2010. I report the average number of citations per paper, the Google Scholar h-index and g-index. In order to get a realistic citations per paper count, I merged duplicate papers, removed book reviews, commentaries, obituaries, conference announcements, call for papers, etc. as these items rarely ever attract citations. Including them would distort comparisons between journals that include these items and journals that do not.

Top-5 accounting journals stand apart

The top-5 accounting journals (all A* ranked in the ABDC ranking) stand apart in terms of their Journal Impact Factor and Google Scholar metrics .However, there is quite a difference in terms of citations per paper for the remaining journals. *European Accounting Review, Accounting and Business Research* and *Journal of Accounting and Public Policy* have a citation per paper rate that is 2-3 times as high as the journals towards the bottom of the list. This is true despite the fact that they were all ranked A on the Australian journal ranking list.

Cites/paper, h-index, and g-index give fairly similar results

The GS h-index and GS g-index also show similar differences. Overall though, there is a very strong correlation between the three GS-based impact measures (0.86 between GS cpp and GS h-index; 0.92 between GS cpp and GS g-index; 0.98 between the h-index and g-index). It is, however, interesting to see that some journals (e.g. *Critical Perspectives on Accounting*) publish a fairly large number of impactful papers, as evidenced by the relatively high h-index and g-index, even though the average number of citations per paper is not very high.

Conclusion

In conclusion, our example shows that even when comparing journals that score similarly in stated preference (peer review) rankings, can have very different impact scores. Given that very few Accounting journals have ISI journal impact factors, a Google Scholar based impact analysis is an excellent way to assess the impact of non-IS listed journals. This would apply equally to journals in many other areas of the Social Sciences and Humanities. A PoP impact analysis for the journal in question thus allows you to make a more-informed choice when you chose a journal to submit your paper to.

Your notes

PoP tip 57: Where to submit your paper? (3): Before submission: Have you missed any papers?

Before submitting to a journal, use Publish or Perish to find out whether the journal you intend to submit to has published any (recent) relevant papers on your topic. You might have missed them whilst you were working hard on the final version of your paper.

Don't annoy the journal editor

There are few things that annoy a journal editor more than to receive a paper for their journal that neglects to refer to relevant papers in the journal in question. I am not talking here about the practice of the less scrupulous amongst the journal editors: asking you to cite papers from their own journal simply to increase their journal's ISI Journal Impact Factor.

Not acknowledging conversation partners is rude

However, journal editors are rightly annoyed if you have failed to incorporate **relevant** prior papers from their journal. By publishing in a certain journal, you are contributing to a conversation. Not acknowledging the other conversation partners is plain rude. So how do you do a final check to establish that you haven't missed any highly relevant papers in the journal you are targeting? You could browse tables of contents on the web or in the library. However, Publish or Perish offers a much quicker way.

Worked example: Entry modes of Japanese MNCs

Let's assume you have written a paper about entry mode choice (the choice between different ways to enter a foreign market) of Japanese multinational companies and intend to submit to *Journal of International Business Studies*.

Use General citation search with "The phrase" and "Publication" fields

Simply search for the term entry mode in the **The phrase** field of the General citation search with "*Journal of International Business Studies*" in the **Publication** field. This will provide any articles in which the words *entry mode* appear in that particular order. If this search provides you with too many results to cope with, you can narrow down your search by clicking the **Title words only** box.

The screenshot below provides **all** articles that have been published in *Journal of International Business Studies* since its inception in 1970 that have entry mode in their title, sorted by number of citations.

Continued interest in this topic in the last 25 years

As you can see the topic of entry modes has generated continued interest from international business scholars in the last 25 years. There is even a discussion going on in the journal as to whether more research on entry mode is needed, something you might like to refer to in your paper.

Cites	Per year	Authors	Title	Year
✓ 𝟔 4756	176.15	B Kogut, H Singh	The effect of national culture on the choice of entry mode	1988
✓ h 1733	75.35	S Agarwal, SN Ra...	Choice of foreign market entry mode: Impact of ownership, location and internalization factors	1992
✓ h 1099	47.78	WC Kim, P Hwang	Global strategy and multinationals' entry mode choice	1992
✓ 𝟔 953	73.31	KD Brouthers	Institutional, cultural and transaction cost influences on entry mode choice and performance	2002
✓ h 705	50.36	KE Meyer	Institutions, transaction costs, and entry mode choice in Eastern Europe	2001
✓ h 656	31.24	CP Woodcock, P...	Ownership-based entry mode strategies and international performance	1994
✓ h 599	59.90	L Tihanyi, DA Grif...	The effect of cultural distance on entry mode choice, international diversification, and MNE perf...	2005
✓ h 394	30.31	JW Lu	Intra-and inter-organizational imitative behavior: Institutional influences on Japanese firms' entr...	2002
✓ h 385	35.00	H Zhao, Y Luo, T ...	Transaction cost determinants and ownership-based entry mode choice: A meta-analytical review	2004
✓ h 378	25.20	PS Davis, AB Des...	Mode of international entry: An isomorphism perspective	2000
✓ h 322	20.13	Y Pan, S Li, DK Tse	The impact of order and mode of market entry on profitability and market share	1999
✓ h 230	28.75	I Filatotchev, R S...	FDI by firms from newly industrialised economies in emerging markets: corporate governance, e...	2007
✓ h 227	28.38	D Dikova, A Van ...	Foreign direct investment mode choice: entry and establishment modes in transition economies	2007
✓ h 205	15.77	P Herrmann, DK D...	CEO successor characteristics and the choice of foreign market entry mode: An empirical study	2002
✓ h 130	10.83	JR Brown, CS De...	Broadening the foreign market entry mode decision: separating ownership and control	2003
✓ h 110	18.33	JF Puck, D Holtbr...	Beyond entry mode choice: Explaining the conversion of joint ventures into wholly owned subsid...	2009
✓ h 46	23.00	KD Brouthers	A retrospective on: Institutional, cultural and transaction cost influences on entry mode choice a...	2013
✓ h 37	18.50	JM Shaver	Do we really need more entry mode studies&quest	2013
✓ h 27	9.00	KK Boeh, PW Bea...	Travel time and the liability of distance in foreign direct investment: Location choice and entry m...	2012
✓ h 20	6.67	B Maekelburger, ...	Asset specificity and foreign market entry mode choice of small and medium-sized enterprises: T...	2012
✓ 19	9.50	X Martin	Solving theoretical and empirical conundrums in international strategy research: Linking foreign e...	2013
✓ 10	10.00	JF Hennart, AHL ...	Yes, we really do need more entry mode studies! A commentary on Shaver	2014

Quick and easy vs. less restrictive search

This is a very quick and easy way to ensure that you haven't missed any papers that might be crucial to your topic. However, it does not allow you to find papers that might provide important insights on entry mode choice, but do not list the words in their title. Hence, you might wish to do a less restrictive search as well and at least eyeball the results. If a less restrictive search provides you with too many results you can also choose to add additional keywords (e.g. Japan, greenfield) that need to occur in the article.

No papers at all?

If your search finds that the journal you intend to submit your paper to has **never** published anything on the topic of your paper or has last published something more than a decade ago, you might wish to reconsider your choice. Remember: You wanting to submit to the journal, because it is the top-ranked journal in your field, is not a good enough reason!

Not an easy way to get a paper accepted

Of course there can be very good reasons to want to introduce a particular stream of research to a new audience, but realize that this is not usually an easy way to get your paper accepted. Academics (and people in general) often find it difficult to relate to ideas that have no connection at all to their knowledge base.

Reviewers and readers might not be able to evaluate your paper's merits

If there is no prior published work on your topic in the journal, reviewers of the journal might not be familiar with this field and might not be able to evaluate its merits. It might also mean that the readers of the journal might not be interested in reading your work, even if it should get accepted. Maybe it is a sign you should take a step back and examine which journals publish on your topic?

PoP tip 58: How to conduct a Literature review search?

To conduct a literature review search you will have to use the Publish or Perish General citation search. Depending on how broad you want the results to be, you could use **Any of the words**, **All of the words** or **The phrase**. This will match these words anywhere in the resulting publications. If you use **The phrase**, the words will be matched in the order they were entered.

"Title words only" identifies key publications

If you want to narrow down the results, ticking the Title words only box will only provide publications where the words are included in the title. As one would normally expect important publications in a field to include relevant key words in their title, this might be a good strategy.

Worked example: Born global firms

Let's assume you would like to know what has been written about the relatively new concept of "born global" firms in international business. Born global firms are firms who start operating internationally from their inception, rather than starting out as domestic firms first and only internationalising gradually.

To do so enter *"born global" OR "born globals"* in **All of the words**, check the **Title words only** box, and leave all subject area boxes checked. I initially conducted this search in 2010. After removing duplicates, this search identified some 150 papers.

When running the same search again in 2015 this had increased to more than 400 papers, three of which have been cited more than 1500 times. The screenshot below shows all papers with more than 400 citations.

Cites		Authors	Title	Year	Publication
☑	h 1565	GA Knight, ST Cavusgil	Innovation, organizational capabilities, and the born-global firm	2004	Journal of International Business ...
☑	h 1554	TK Madsen, P Servais	The internationalization of born globals: an evolutionary process?	1997	International business review
☑	h 1510	GA Knight, ST Cavusgil	The born global firm: A challenge to traditional internationalization theory	1996	Advances in international marketing
☑	h 841	MW Rennie	Born global	1993	The McKinsey Quarterly
☑	h 624	DD Sharma, A Blomstermo	The internationalization process of born globals: a network view	2003	International business review
☑	h 604	Ø Moen, P Servais	Born global or gradual global? Examining the export behavior of small a...	2002	Journal of international marketing
☑	h 563	S Chetty, C Campbell-Hunt	A strategic approach to internationalization: a traditional versus a "bor...	2004	Journal of International Marketing
☑	h 547	L Zhou, W Wu, X Luo	Internationalization and the performance of born-global SMEs: the me...	2007	Journal of International Business ...
☑	h 467	Ø Moen	The born globals: a new generation of small European exporters	2002	International Marketing Review
☑	h 452	J Bell, R McNaughton, S Y...	'Born-again global' firms: An extension to the 'born global' phenomenon	2001	Journal of International Managem...
☑	h 430	S Andersson, I Wictor	Innovative internationalisation in new firms: born globals—the Swedish ...	2003	Journal of International Entrepren...

Your notes

PoP tip 59: Identifying the key authors, journals, and publications in a field of research

In addition to doing a quick general search on what has been published in a particular field, Publish or Perish can also be used to do a more in-depth literature search.

- You can for instance find out who the founding fathers (or mothers) of a particular field are.

- You can establish how the research field has developed since its origins.

- You can learn what the journals are in which academics most frequently publish about this topic.

- Finally, once you have found a key publication in the field, you can do further research following up on this publication.

Founding fathers

Going back to our earlier example about born global firms, sorting the results by year allows us to identify the "founding author(s)" of the concept. Below I have reproduced all articles with born global in the title until 2000; the first publication was in 1993 by MW Rennie in *McKinsey Quarterly*.

Cites		Authors	Title	Year
✓ *h*	841	MW Rennie	Born global	1993
✓	29	ST Cavusgil	Born globals: a quiet revolution among Australian exporters	1994
✓	0	J Laing	The 'Born Global' Wine Producer -Overcoming the Tyranny of Distance	1995
✓ *h*	1510	GA Knight, ST Cavusgil	The born global firm: A challenge to traditional internationalization ...	1996
✓ *h*	1554	TK Madsen, P Servais	The internationalization of born globals: an evolutionary process?	1997
✓ *h*	235	GA Knight	Emerging paradigm for international marketing: The born global firm	1997
✓	41	ST Cavusgil, GA Knight	Explaining an Emerging Phenomenon for International Marketing: ...	1997
✓	50	S Kandasaami	Internationalisation of small-and medium-sized born-global firms: a...	1998
✓	5	C Gurău, A Ranchhod	The 'Born Global' firms in UK biotechnology	1999
✓	4	P Servais, ES Rasmussen	Born Globals—connectors between various industrial districts	1999
✓ *h*	235	PD Harveston, BL Kedia, P...	Internationalization of born global and gradual globalizing firms: T...	2000
✓ *h*	206	TK Madsen, E Rasmussen,....	Differences and similarities between born globals and other types ...	2000
✓ *h*	101	E Autio, HJ Sapienza	Comparing process and born global perspectives in the internation...	2000
✓ *h*	69	PD Harveston	Synoptic versus incremental internationalization: An examination o...	2000
✓ *h*	58	J Bell, R McNAUGHTON	Born global firms: a challenge to public policy in support of internat...	2000
✓	35	S Kandasaami, X Huang	International marketing strategy of SMEs. A comparison of born-gl...	2000
✓	27	T Almor	Born global: the case of small and medium sized, knowledge-intens...	2000
✓	21	G Knight, TK Madsen, P S...	The born global firm: description and empirical investigation in Eur...	2000
✓	9	PD Harveston, BL Kedia, P...	Internationalization of born global and gradual globalizing firms: th...	2000
✓	7	V Sasi, M Gabrielsson, M ...	Financing and Managing Growth of A Born Global: Case of Mad. O...	2000
✓	3	S Saarenketo, TS Äijö	Born Globals—conceptualization and empirical illustrations	2000

The paper talks about a McKinsey study amongst Australian firms that identified small and medium-sized companies that successfully competed against large, established players in the global arena without first building a home base. Hence, a consulting firm in Australia first discovered the phenomenon.

- Second publication by well-known marketing academic

The second publication is an editorial by a well-known academic in International Marketing, who – in the *Journal of International Marketing* – reports on the results of the McKinsey study that he discovered when spending 6 months as a Fulbright Scholar in Australia. Cavusgil (1994:4) says: *"I would like to comment on an interesting phenomenon in the Australian export scene. It is relevant to those of us in other post-industrial economies and, hopefully, should spur some research interests."*

- Third publication has sunk without a citation trace

Interestingly, the third publication is also about Australian born globals, this time wine producers. However, even after 20 years, the article hasn't generated a single citation. This seems to suggest it has not been picked by researchers, no doubt largely caused by the fact that it was published in a rather obscure and specialized journal (*Australian and New Zealand Wine Industry Journal*).

- Working papers can be influential too

The Australian angle is also apparent in a later conceptual paper by Kandasaami at the University of Western Australia in 1998. Interestingly, this paper did gather nearly 50 citations, despite being an unpublished working paper.

Historical development of the field

Cavusgil took his own recommendation to heart and started researching this phenomenon, leading to a very highly cited publication in 1996 – co-authored with Gary Knight – in the research annual *Advances in International Marketing*. Both Knight and Cavusgil went on to publish many other papers in this field.

- Danish interest at an early stage

They were joined at an early stage by Danish academic Tage Madsen, who, with his Danish co-authors Servais and Rasmussen, published a number of papers on the topic. In 1999, the phenomenon was also picked up in the UK, where Gurau & Ranchhod researched biotechnology firms.

- More interest from academics in small peripheral economies

By 2000 the topic had spread to researchers in the USA (Harveston et al.), Ireland (Bell), Finland (Autio, Sasi, Saarenketo), and Israel (Almor). Interest remained strong amongst researchers these countries, but after 2000 they were joined by researchers in Sweden, Portugal, and New Zealand. With the exception of some researchers in the USA and Israel, the phenomenon thus initially attracted most interest from academics in "small" economies at the peripheries of the world.

- Expansion to bigger European, Latin American and Asian countries

The mid 2000s saw the interest in the phenomenon expand to countries such as Germany, Switzerland, Mexico, Korea, with Latin American countries (Brazil, Columbia, Costa Rica) and Italy joining from the late 2000s. In the early 2010s the geographical interest had spread to India, China, and Eastern Europe.

The year 2012 saw the publication of a *Handbook of Research on Born Globals* with 18 chapters by different researchers in the field, as well as an annotated bibliography. In 2015, the 2014 JIBS decade award went to Knight's and Cavusgil's paper on *"Innovation, organizational capabilities, and the born-global firm"*. In the same year, Gary Knight published a review article (*"Born global firms: Evolution of a contemporary phenomenon"*) in *Advances in International Marketing*. It appears that after 20 years, the topic of "born globals" has reached maturity.

Important journals

Sorting our earlier results on born global firms by publication allows us to identify the journals that publish articles relating to this topic.

- Mainstream International Business journals

All of the mainstream international business journals (*Journal of International Business Studies, Journal of World Business, Management International Review,* and *International Business Review*) contained a substantial number of papers on the topic.

- Specialized International Marketing journals

Specialized International Marketing journals such as *International Marketing Review* and *Journal of International Marketing* also contain a large number of papers on this topic. Most born global firms are exporters rather than multinationals with subsidiaries abroad. Exporting has traditionally been a topic of interest to the International Marketing community.

- Entrepreneurship journals

Finally, the results also show a large number of papers in the *International Journal of Globalisation and Small Business* and a very large number of papers in the *Journal of International Entrepreneurship*. This illustrates that the born global phenomenon often concerns small and medium sized firms and that the early internationalization decision should be seen in the context of entrepreneurship.

Follow up on key publications in the field

Your literature review will discover the seminal publications in the field. These could be publications that are highly cited or publications that deal with exactly the topic you are interested in. Normally, you will want to ensure that you also review papers citing this seminal piece of work. These papers will often show up in your initial search, but if they look at the phenomenon from a different angle and don't refer to the exact same concepts, they will not be captured.

Use Lookup citations to find articles citing seminal publications

So how can you use Publish or Perish to follow up on publications that cite your seminal publications? Simply right-click on the seminal work and chose **Lookup citations**. This will look all referring works and present them ordered by the number of citations. The screenshot below shows the ten most highly cited articles that cite the first publication on born globals (Rennie 1996). Of these, six were already included in our initial search, as they have born global in the title.

Cites	Authors	Title
✓ h 2525	J Alba, J Lynch, B Weitz, …	Interactive home shopping: consumer, retailer, and manufacturer incentives to participate in electronic marketplaces
✓ h 1574	GA Knight, ST Cavusgil	Innovation, organizational capabilities, and the born-global firm
✓ h 1559	TK Madsen, P Servais	The internationalization of born globals: an evolutionary process?
✓ h 1241	JA Quelch, LR Klein	The Internet and international marketing
✓ h 791	A Rialp, J Rialp, GA Knight	The phenomenon of early internationalizing firms: what do we know after a decade (1993–2003) of scientific inquiry?
✓ h 681	MV Jones, NE Coviello	Internationalisation: conceptualising an entrepreneurial process of behaviour in time
✓ h 628	DD Sharma, A Blomstermo	The internationalization process of born globals: a network view
✓ h 606	Ø Moen, P Servais	Born global or gradual global? Examining the export behavior of small and medium-sized enterprises
✓ h 565	S Chetty, C Campbell-Hunt	A strategic approach to internationalization: a traditional versus a "born-global" approach
✓ h 548	L Zhou, W Wu, X Luo	Internationalization and the performance of born-global SMEs: the mediating role of social networks

Of the remaining articles, those by Alba et al. and Quelch & Klein are probably not very relevant. However, the publications by Rialp, Rialp & Knight and Jones & Covielo appear highly relevant, even though they do not mention the terms born global in the title.

Conclusion

Publish or Perish can help you do detailed literature review on a key topic, reviewing the topic's origins and development, as well as the key journals and authors in the field.

PoP tip 60: Development of the literature over time

Publish or Perish can also be used to analyse the development of the literature on a particular topic over time. Using the **General citation search** function you can search for particular key words and look at how the number of papers published varies over time.

Limit your search by journal to eliminate irrelevant results

To eliminate a potentially large range of irrelevant results it is a good idea to focus on a small set of journals. Journals can be combined with the OR function in the publication field, although Google Scholar generally ignores any journals beyond the second or third.

Export for further analyses in a spread sheet or statistical program

Publish or Perish does not yet provide the ability to further analyse for instance the number of publications per year. However, exporting the data to a spread sheet or statistical program allows you to do this very easily. In addition, by selecting all publications in a year, clicking "unselect" and looking at the reduction in the number of papers, you can easily establish the number of papers per year.

Worked Example: Culture in the field of International Business

Let us assume you are interested how research into national culture in the field of business and management has developed over the years. To limit the number of irrelevant hits, you limit your search to two mainstream international business journals. The screenshot below shows the search and all papers receiving more than 300 citations.

- What are the most highly cited papers?

The most cited paper – by a large distance – is Kogut & Singh's paper on the effect of national culture on the choice of entry mode. This was a seminal paper in that it introduced culture as a variable to be considered in studies on entry modes. Other highly cited papers are those providing reviews of the field (e.g. Adler, Hofstede, & Leung et al.).

- Impact of culture on managerial work values and practices

However, the general study of the impact of culture on managerial work values and practices is also popular (Newman & Nollen; Ralston et al.). Further highly cited papers deal with the impact of culture on specific topics such as corruption (Husted), strategy (Hennart & Larimo), entrepreneurship (Thomas & Mueller), compensation practices (Schuler & Rogovsky), and business negotiations (Graham).

- Interest in the role of culture is increasing over time

When I sort the articles by year, I find the interest in the role of culture to be increasing. There were only six articles published in the 1980s that had culture in their title. Likewise, in the first half of the nineties, only five articles dealt with culture to such an extent that they included the word in their title. In the latter half of the nineties, the number of articles published on culture increased to nearly a dozen. The first decade of the 21st century produced some 40 articles on culture, with another 40 published in the next five years. It is clear that culture is a topic that is of sustained interest to international business scholars!

Author(s):	
Publication:	"Journal of International Business Studies" OR "International Business Review"
Journal ISSN:	
All of the words:	
Any of the words:	
None of the words:	
The phrase:	culture
Year of publication between:	0 and: 0 ☑ Title words only
Data source:	Google Scholar ▼

Results

Papers:	145	Cites/paper:	120.76	h-index:	51	"Journal of International Business Studie
Citations:	17510	Cites/author:	9041.27	g-index:	132	Query date: 2015-12-21
Years:	32	Papers/author:	84.98	hI,norm:	38	Papers: 145
Cites/year:	547.19	Authors/paper:	2.15	hI,annual:	1.19	Citations: 17510
						Years: 32

Cites		Authors	Title	Year
☑ *h*	4746	B Kogut, H Singh	The effect of national culture on the choice of entry mode	1988
☑ *h*	1047	KL Newman, SD Nollen	Culture and congruence: The fit between management practice...	1996
☑ *h*	742	K Leung, RS Bhagat, NR...	Culture and international business: Recent advances and their i...	2005
☑ *h*	737	DA Ralston, DH Holt, RH...	The impact of national culture and economic ideology on manag...	1997
☑ *h*	659	BW Husted...	Wealth, culture, and corruption	1999
☑ *h*	647	G Hofstede	The business of international business is culture	1994
☑ *h*	637	AS Thomas, SL Mueller	A case for comparative entrepreneurship: Assessing the releva...	2000
☑ *h*	631	NJ Adler	A typology of management studies involving culture	1983
☑ *h*	513	JF Hennart, J Larimo	The impact of culture on the strategy of multinational enterpris...	1998
☑ *h*	412	RS Schuler, N Rogovsky	Understanding compensation practice variations across firms: T...	1998
☑ *h*	378	V Pothukuchi, F Damanp...	National and organizational culture differences and internationa...	2002
☑ *h*	311	JL Graham	The influence of culture on the process of business negotiations...	1985

Worked example: HIV in Science, Nature and Cell

Let us assume you are interested on how research on HIV has developed over the years. You focus your search on three core journals that are likely to publish on this topic: Science, Nature and Cell. You would then run the following query.

Author(s):	
Publication:	Science OR Nature OR Cell
Journal ISSN:	
All of the words:	
Any of the words:	
None of the words:	
The phrase:	HIV
Year of publication between:	0 and: 0 ☑ Title words only

The screenshot below shows all papers with more than 2,000 citations. We can see that each of the three journals has published highly cited articles in this field: four in Cell, six in Nature and eight in Science. We can also observe that most of the highly cited articles were published between 1995 and 1997, and in fact 11 out of the 18 most highly cited articles were published in 1996.

Cites		Authors	Title	Year	Publication
✓	h 4456	DD Ho, AU Neumann, AS Perelson,...	Rapid turnover of plasma virions and CD4 lymphocytes in HIV-1...	1995	Nature
✓	h 4385	Y Feng, CC Broder, PE Kennedy, E...	HIV-1 entry cofactor: functional cDNA cloning of a seven-trans...	1996	Science
✓	h 3790	HK Deng, R Liu, W Ellmeier, S Choe...	Identification of a major co-receptor for primary isolates of HIV-1	1996	Nature
✓	h 3336	T Dragic, V Litwin, GP Allaway, SR ...	HIV-1 entry into CD4 sup+ cells is mediated by the chemokine r...	1996	Nature
✓	h 3125	AS Perelson, AU Neumann, M Mark...	HIV-1 dynamics in vivo: virion clearance rate, infected cell life-s...	1996	Science
✓	h 3064	F Cocchi, AL DeVico, A Garzino-De...	Identification of RANTES, MIP-1α, and MIP-1β as the major HI...	1995	Science
✓	h 2939	G Alkhatib, C Combadiere, CC Brod...	CC CKR5: a RANTES, MIP-1α, MIP-1β receptor as a fusion cofa...	1996	Science
✓	h 2845	R Liu, WA Paxton, S Choe, D Cera...	Homozygous defect in HIV-1 coreceptor accounts for resistanc...	1996	Cell
✓	h 2820	PD Kwong, R Wyatt, J Robinson, R...	Structure of an HIV gp120 envelope glycoprotein in complex wi...	1998	Nature
✓	h 2755	M Samson, F Libert, BJ Doranz, J R...	Resistance to HIV-1 infection in caucasian individuals bearing m...	1996	Nature
✓	h 2692	JW Mellors, CR Rinaldo, P Gupta, R...	Prognosis in HIV-1 infection predicted by the quantity of virus i...	1996	Science
✓	h 2449	M Dean, M Carrington, C Winkler, ...	Genetic restriction of HIV-1 infection and progression to AIDS b...	1996	Science
✓	h 2401	H Choe, M Farzan, Y Sun, N Sulliva...	The β-chemokine receptors CCR3 and CCR5 facilitate infection ...	1996	Cell
✓	h 2209	TBH Geijtenbeek, DS Kwon, R Tore...	DC-SIGN, a dendritic cell–specific HIV-1-binding protein that en...	2000	Cell
✓	h 2177	DC Chan, D Fass, JM Berger, PS Kim	Core structure of gp41 from the HIV envelope glycoprotein	1997	Cell
✓	h 2119	JM Coffin	HIV population dynamics in vivo: implications for genetic variati...	1995	Science
✓	h 2093	D Finzi, M Hermankova, T Pierson, ...	Identification of a reservoir for HIV-1 in patients on highly activ...	1997	Science
✓	h 2084	CC Bleul, M Farzan, H Choe, C Par...	The lymphocyte chemoattractant SDF-1 is a ligand for LESTR/f...	1996	Nature

- Development of research volume over time

However, I am also interested in how the volume of research on HIV has developed over the years. In order to assess this, I rerun the search for a single journal: Science. The reason for this is that if I include all journals only the most highly cited 1000 results will be shown and this will naturally include fewer recent articles.

- Splitting a search into two to include all papers

Running the search for Science alone, splitting it in into two time periods (before and after 1996) and aggregating both searches into one ensures I also include less-cited articles (there are 100+ articles without citations in both periods). This reduces the risk of missing most of the recently published articles.

- Number of publications on HIV peak in 1988

When I sort the results by year, I find that articles on HIV started to be published in Science in 1986. However, after removing duplicates, I found only four articles published in that year. About a dozen articles were published in 1987, whilst nearly 50 articles were published in 1988. This was one of the years with the largest number of publications on HIV in Science.

- Another peak in publications in 1996

Between 1989 and 1995 the number of articles had gone down to about 20-30. However, in 1996 the number of articles reached nearly 50 again, dropping to around 30 again in 1997-1999. From the early 2000s, the number of articles published on HIV in Science went down to about 15 a year, with a seeming resurgence from 2013 onwards where we see a return to 25-30 articles a year.

- Publication peaks follow major medical developments

The name HIV was introduced in May 1986 by the International Committee on the Taxonomy of Viruses. The current treatment for HIV was introduced in 1996, resulting in a declining number of deaths from HIV/AIDS. Studying the scientific interest in HIV (or any illness) thus allows one to understand the development of interest in the disease over time.

Your notes

PoP tip 61: Bibliometric research with Google Scholar

There are now many bibliometric studies that rely on Google Scholar (with Publish or Perish) to do their research. An **all of the words** Google Scholar search for the words: *Harzing "Publish or Perish"* results in nearly 2,000 hits.

Google Scholar has come a long way...

Google Scholar has come a long way since the early days of its introduction in 2004. Its coverage has improved dramatically and is now better for all disciplines than either the Web of Science or Scopus. The table below summarises part of the results of our recent study of 146 academics in the Life Sciences, Sciences, Engineering, Social Sciences and Humanities.

- Harzing, A.W.; Alakangas, S. (2016) **Google Scholar, Scopus and the Web of Science: A longitudinal and cross-disciplinary comparison**, in press for *Scientometrics*. Available online... - Publisher's version - Presentation slides - Video presentation of this article.

Discipline	Scopus citations as % of Google Scholar citations	Web of Science citations as % of Google Scholar citations
Humanities	11.5%	7.0%
Social Sciences	30.0%	22.7%
Engineering	57.6%	45.7%
Sciences	64.2%	65.6%
Life Sciences	70.5%	66.8%

As is immediately apparent, both the Web of Science and Scopus miss a huge number of citations in the Humanities and Social Sciences, mostly because they do include book publications and in some disciplines cover only a fraction of the journals. However, even in Engineering, the Sciences and the Life Sciences, Google Scholar reports between one-and-a-half and twice as many citations as the Web of Science and Scopus.

Google Scholar is not a bibliometric database

However, just like Publish or Perish, Google Scholar is free and does not charge any subscription fees. Its data rely on crawling websites with scholarly articles. Thus one cannot expect the same level of accuracy as manually curated databases such as the Web of Science and Scopus that charge universities a very hefty subscription fee.

Sacrifice a little accuracy for a lot more comprehensive coverage

That said, based on my own and other recent research on Google Scholar I would estimate that - ignoring the [citation] records - its accuracy lies above 95%. Scopus and the Web of Science probably have an accuracy level of above 99%, but the comprehensiveness of their coverage is **much** lower than Google Scholar.

Doing bibliometric research on authors or journals

The next two tips provide you with some suggestions on how to do bibliometric research on author or journals. They use Google Scholar as a data source. However, Publish or Perish can import ISI/Web of Science and Scopus data as well, so if you prefer you can conduct the same studies with different data sources.

PoP tip 62: Doing bibliometric research for authors

Publish or Perish can be used to do systematic bibliometric research for authors. The key question in this type of study is what population of authors to include. Of course this is largely dependent on your research question.

Comparing data sources and metrics across disciplines

If your aim is to study the impact of different data sources or different metrics for comparisons across disciplines, you will obviously need to select academics from a broad range of disciplines. This is what we did in this paper where we compared 146 academics across the Sciences, Life Sciences, Engineering, Social Sciences and Humanities.

- Harzing, A.W.; Alakangas, S. (2016) **Google Scholar, Scopus and the Web of Science: A longitudinal and cross-disciplinary comparison**, in press for *Scientometrics*. Available online... - Publisher's version - Presentation slides - Video presentation of this article.

The screenshot below shows a small part of the multi-query centre folders that were created for this project.

Creating rankings of individual academics

However, most academics that are using Publish or Perish to do bibliometric research intend to create some sort of ranking of individual academics. This necessitates a more focused population. The following options are possible.

- ### Pick a specific discipline

In order for a ranking to make any sense to your readers, it is usually best to limit your population by discipline. However, even within disciplines there can be very substantial differences in typical citation scores. Hence your definition of discipline might need to be fairly narrow.

The authors' data management and search procedures are exemplary. Anyone wanting to conduct bibliometric research on authors would be well advised to read their paper. The paper also has an excellent supplementary page with career-stage impact calculators, additional analyses and search tips.

- Nosek, B. A., Graham, J., Lindner, N. M., Kesebir, S., Hawkins, C. B., Hahn, C., ... & Tenney, E. R. (2010). Cumulative and career-stage citation impact of social-personality psychology programs and their members. *Personality and Social Psychology Bulletin, 36*(10), 1283-1300.

- Pick a specific country

An additional way to narrow down your population is by country. This both limits the scope of the data collection effort and reduces differences caused by different research traditions in different countries. As most studies aim to produce norm scores of some sort, this is a good thing. Obviously, if your research question is to compare the impact of different research traditions on citation patterns, your choice would be different.

- Pick academics who share specific attributes

As even narrowing down the population by discipline or country can leave you with a very large number of academics, most studies narrow down their field even further by studying academics that share specific attributes. These attributes could for instance be:
- Working at the top 5/10/20 universities (however defined) in the country
- Being a fellow of one of the major professional association in the discipline
- Being editor or editorial board member of one of journals in the discipline
- Having been president of a major professional association in the field
- Having won a major research award (e.g. dissertation award, Nobel prize)
- Having done their PhD at a specific set of institutions.

Obviously, your selection would need to make sense in the context of your research questions. There are only so many simple exploratory ranking studies that can be published, even if you are personally very interested in the results.

PoP tip 63: Doing bibliometric research for journals: investigating co-authorship patterns

In addition to calculating the impact of specific journals or articles, Publish or Perish can also be used to compare a specific set of journals on a number of characteristics or test specific hypotheses on topics such as research collaborations.

Country differences in co-authorship patterns

Let's assume for instance that I want to test the hypothesis that on average North Americans tend to publish more co-authored papers than Europeans. I could conduct a large-scale comparison of North American versus European academics. However, that would be quite time-consuming.

- Use journal-level stats to investigate authorship patterns

I can also investigate this on a journal level, as it has been well established that North American journals tend to have a larger proportion of North American authors, whilst European journals have a large proportion of European authors. This tends to be true in any discipline, but it is certainly the case the Social Sciences and Humanities whose research topics tend to be more location-bound than the Sciences.

- Accounting: on average articles in US journals have more co-authors

Taking Accounting journals as an example, of the six ISI-listed journals, four are North America (JAR, AR, CAR and RAS), whilst the remaining two journals *Accounting, Organizations and Society* and *European Accounting Review* are European. As shown in the screenshot below, with Publish or Perish statistics exported to Excel, co-authorship patterns do indeed differ between the North American (2.07-2.34 authors per paper) and the European journals (1.71-1.87 authors per paper).

	A	B	C	D	E	F	G	H	I	J	K
					Cites	Cites	Cites A	Papers	Authors	h_ind	g_ind
1	Query	Papers	Citation	Yea	Yea	Pap	utho	Autho	Pape	ex	ex
2	Accounting Review, 1558-7967: all	903	112022	16	7001	124.06	57976	473.12	2.34	173	303
3	Journal of Accounting Research, 1475-67	481	59913	14	4280	124.56	29929	271.75	2.2	126	233
4	Review of Accounting Studies, 1573-713	487	34016	19	1790	69.85	16777	279.45	2.2	92	170
5	Contemporary Accounting Research, 19:	927	59978	31	1935	64.7	33989	556.7	2.07	111	216
6	European Accounting Review, 1468-449	744	37420	23	1627	50.3	24097	497.57	1.87	104	155
7	Accounting, Organizations and Society, (	935	155512	39	3987	166.32	111243	666.47	1.71	208	339

- The same pattern is found in other disciplines

Of course this is only a very small sample of journals, but one could easily expand this to other journals in Accounting or Business in general and the same general pattern will be likely to be found. For instance, if one compares *Organization Science* and *Organization Studies*, two journals in the field of Management with a very similar research domain, I find that, on average, the US-based journal has a larger number of authors per paper than the European journal, even when the latter's many single-authored book reviews are excluded.

Co-authorship patterns across disciplines and time

This same strategy can also be used to compare co-authorship patterns across disciplines and time. One could for instance take the top-3 journals in every discipline and calculate co-authorship patterns, rather than having to rely on a sample of academics in these disciplines. Doing this, one could not just look at the average number of authors per paper, but also at the number of paper with 1, 2, 3, and more authors as well as the modal number of authors per paper.

- Different co-authorship patterns in Sciences, Social Sciences and Humanities

A very small-scale comparison looking at co-authorship patterns for articles published in the above two Management journals between 1995-2014 with two top journals in the Sciences and the Humanities already shows very interesting results.

Journal Title	Mean 1995-1999	Mean 2000-2004	Mean 2005-2009	Mean 2010-2014	Mode
Environmental History	1.00	1.00	1.06	1.06	1, 1, 1,1
Evolutionary Anthropology	1.29	1.54	1.53	1.75	1, 1, 1, 1
Organization Studies	1.66	1.76	1.84	2.05	1, 1, 1, 2
Organization Science	1.84	2.04	2.28	2.30	2, 2, 2, 2
Nature Genetics	4.74	4.80	4.98	5.32	5, 5, 5, 5
Nature Medicine	4.65	4.69	5.02	4.81	5, 5, 5, 5

- Modal number of authors varies from 1 to 5 across disciplines

Whilst in the Humanities sole authorship is the norm, in the Sciences papers typically have a much larger number of authors. Management – as one of the Social Sciences – falls between these extremes, but is much closer to the Humanities than to the Sciences.

- Knowledge of disciplinary differences can help in promotion case

Obviously, these results can be useful if one wants to make a case for promotion to a panel that is comprised of academics from different disciplines. It helps to explain why it is not realistic to expect the same number of publications from academics in the Social Sciences and Humanities as from academics in the Sciences.

- Number of co-authors is increasing over time for all disciplines

Another hypothesis that we could test is whether the number of co-authors tends to increase over time, reflecting the more collaborative nature of academic research and publishing in more recent times. The table above clearly shows that, even though the modal number of authors hasn't changed for most journals, overall there has been an increase in the number of authors per paper over time for all three disciplines.

PoP tip 64: Google Scholar: strengths and weaknesses

Publish or Perish uses Google Scholar as its database. This means that any advantages and disadvantages that are present in Google Scholar will also be present in Publish or Perish. If you prefer to work with ISI/Web of Science data or Scopus data, you can use ISI Import or Scopus Import.

Google Scholar has come a long way...

Google Scholar has come a long way since the early days of its introduction in 2004. Its coverage has improved dramatically and is now better for all disciplines than either the Web of Science or Scopus. As a result there are now many bibliometric studies that rely on Google Scholar (with Publish or Perish) to do their research. An **all of the words** Google Scholar search for the words: *Harzing "Publish or Perish"* results in nearly 2,000 hits.

Google Scholar is not a bibliometric database

However, just like Publish or Perish, Google Scholar is free and does not charge any subscription fees. Its data rely on crawling websites with scholarly articles. Thus one cannot expect the same level of accuracy as manually curated databases such as the Web of Science and Scopus, that charge universities a very hefty subscription fee.

Sacrifice a little accuracy for a lot more comprehensive coverage

That said, based on my own and other recent research on Google Scholar I would estimate that - ignoring the [citation] records - its accuracy lies above 95%. Scopus and the Web of Science probably have an accuracy level of above 99%, but the comprehensiveness of their coverage is **much** lower than Google Scholar.

Discipline	Scopus citations as % of Google Scholar citations	Web of Science citations as % of Google Scholar citations
Humanities	11.5%	7.0%
Social Sciences	30.0%	22.7%
Engineering	57.6%	45.7%
Sciences	64.2%	65.6%
Life Sciences	70.5%	66.8%

As is immediately apparent, both the Web of Science and Scopus miss a huge number of citations in the Humanities and Social Sciences, mostly because they do not include book publications and in some disciplines cover only a fraction of the journals. However, even in Engineering, the Sciences and the Life Sciences, Google Scholar reports between one-and-a-half and twice as many citations as the Web of Science and Scopus.

However, there are a number of "quirks"

Google Scholar suffers from a number of limitations that are discussed in the next 10 tips.

Truncation	Book edition cites
Wrong master record	Missing subject areas
Wrong author(s)	Citation years
Inconsistent year	Slow searches
Stray citations	CAPTCHAS

References

- Harzing, A.W.; Alakangas, S. (2016) **Google Scholar, Scopus and the Web of Science: A longitudinal and cross-disciplinary comparison**, in press for *Scientometrics*.
- Harzing, A.W. (2014) **A longitudinal study of Google Scholar coverage between 2012 and 2013**, *Scientometrics*, vol. 98, no. 1, pp. 565-575.
- Harzing, A.W.; Alakangas, S.; Adams, D. (2014) **hIa: An individual annual h-index to accommodate disciplinary and career length differences**, *Scientometrics*, vol. 99, no. 3, pp. 811-821.
- Harzing, A.W. (2013) **A preliminary test of Google Scholar as a source for citation data: A longitudinal study of Nobel Prize winners**, *Scientometrics*, vol. 93, no. 3, pp. 1057-1075.

PoP tip 65: Google Scholar limitations (1): Truncating author and journal names

In the early days, Google Scholar provided complete records for authors and the publication source. However, since about 2012 both fields are regularly truncated, with part of the field replaced by dots [.....].

Truncation makes finding the right publication frustrating

We do not know why Google Scholar decided to do this. It might be related to the "space" available in these fields. Unfortunately it can make finding the right publication very frustrating, both in the Google Scholar interface and in Publish or Perish:

- Sometimes the name of the author one is searching for does not seem to appear in the record at all, because it is replaced by dots.
- With common journal names, it becomes impossible to distinguish in which journal an article is published. *European journal of....* and *International journal of....* could be one of many hundreds of titles.

Author truncation

There does not seem to any particular logic to author truncation. Sometimes four or more authors are shown in full, in other cases the 2nd of two authors is truncated. That said; if one normally co-author with only one or two others, author truncation is generally not very problematic. Out of the 25 co-authored publications in my h-index, only three were truncated, and the 20 single-authored ones are also shown in full.

Journal truncation

The logic to journal truncation seems even more obscure. Similar to authors, some journals with long names are written in full, whereas some shorter ones are truncated. However, as the first screenshot shows, the same journal can also be truncated in many different ways.

2004	International Journal of ...	ccm.sagepub.com
2004	International Journal of Cross ...	ccm.sagepub.com
2006	International Journal of Cross Cultural ...	ccm.sagepub.com
2005	International Journal of Cross Cultural ...	ccm.sagepub.com

Below, out of two articles in the same issue of a journal, one was shown with the full name and the other with a truncated journal name.

2015	Human Resource ...	Wiley Online Library
2007	Human Resource ...	Wiley Online Library
2007	Human Resource Management	Wiley Online Library
2001	Human Resource Management	Wiley Online Library

Author & journal truncation combined

Journal titles appear to be more likely to be truncated when there are more authors or authors with longer names, so it seems likely that Google Scholar applies a limit to the maximum number of characters to the two field combined.

Google Scholar support

If you would like to see truncation removed, let Google Scholar know. Obviously, there is no guarantee they will listen, but we can always try...

http://support.google.com/scholar/bin/request.py?contact_type=general

PoP tip 66: Google Scholar limitations (2):
The wrong master record

No less than 19 versions of the same record

Many publications have multiple occurrences on the Web. For instance my 2009 article with Nancy Adler occurs no less than 19 times.

> **When knowledge wins: Transcending the sense and nonsense of academic rankings**
> NJ Adler, AW Harzing - Academy of Management Learning & ..., 2009 - amle.aom.org
> Has university scholarship gone astray? Do our academic assessment systems reward scholarship
> that addresses the questions that matter most to society? Using international business as an
> example, we highlight the problematic nature of academic ranking systems and question ...
> Cited by 442   Related articles   All 19 versions   Cite   Save

Google usually identifies the correct master record

In nearly all cases, Google Scholar correctly identifies the most appropriate record – usually on the official publisher's website – as the "master record" to which all citations are ascribed. In this case, this is the website of the Academy of Management's journal *Academy of Management Learning & Education.*

Sometimes Google Scholar gets it wrong, very wrong

However, in an estimated 2-3% of the publications, Google Scholar – for unknown reasons – "picks" the wrong record as master record, even if a more appropriate one is available. The article below occurs 15 times, but Google Scholar somehow picked the "worst" master record, a pdf on http.tarma.com that when clicking on it provides a "404 file not found".

> [PDF] **Google Scholar: the democratization of citation analysis**
> AW Harzing, R Van der Wal - Ethics in science and environmental ..., 2007 - http.tarma.com
> Abstract Traditionally, the most commonly used source of bibliometric data is Thomson ISI
> Web of Knowledge, in particular the (Social) Science Citation Index and the Journal Citation
> Reports (JCR), which provide the yearly Journal Impact Factors (JIF). This paper presents ...
> Cited by 374   Related articles   All 15 versions   Cite   Save   More

Even if a "perfect" version is available

A full-text pre-publication version of this article is available from no less than seven sources; even the published version is available from four different sources, including the publisher's website (see below):

> [PDF] **Google Scholar as a new source for citation analysis**
> AWK Harzing, R van der Wal - 2008 - int-res.com
> ABSTRACT: Traditionally, the most commonly used source of bibliometric data is Thomson
> ISI Web of Knowledge, in particular the Web of Science and the Journal Citation Reports
> (JCR), which provide the yearly Journal Impact Factors (JIF). This paper presents an ...
> Cite

Wrong master record presents wrong year and wrong title

As a result of the wrongly attributed master record this publication appears in Google Scholar (and Publish or Perish) not only with the wrong title (the title was changed in the final revision), but also with the wrong publication year. Fortunately, these problems are rare, especially with journal articles published by mainstream publishers.

Your notes

PoP tip 67: Google Scholar limitations (3): Wrong author names

Author missing on co-authored paper

Sometimes Google Scholar does not seem to parse the author field correctly and the publication cannot be found under the name of the author, or one of the authors, even though it can be found by searching by title. For instance, Isabel Metz and I published a paper in *Management International Review* on geographical diversity in editorial boards.

- Harzing, A.W.; Metz, I. (2013) **Practicing what we preach: The geographic diversity of editorial boards**, *Management International Review*, vol. 53, no. 2, pp. 169-187.

Publication shows up for co-author and title search

The publication shows up fine when searching for my name or when searching for the title (see screenshots).

Author impact analysis - Perform a citation analysis for one or more authors

Author's name: "a harzing"

Exclude these authors:

Year of publication between: 0 and: 0

Data source: Google Scholar

Results

Papers:	300	Cites/paper:	32.46	h-index:	45	"a harzing": all
Citations:	9737	Cites/author:	7214.82	g-index:	96	Query date: 2016-01-08
Years:	21	Papers/author:	216.01	hI,norm:	37	Papers: 300 / Citations: 9737
Cites/year:	463.67	Authors/paper:	1.78	hI,annual:	1.76	Years: 21

Cites		Per year	Authors	Title	Year	Publication
☑	18	6.00	AW Harzing	Practicing what we preach	2013	Management International Review

General citation search - Perform a general citation search

Author(s):

Publication: "Management International Review"

Journal ISSN:

All of the words:

Any of the words: |

None of the words:

The phrase: Practicing what we preach

Year of publication between: 0 and: 0   ☑ Title words only

Data source: Google Scholar

Results

Papers:	1	Cites/paper:	18.00	h-index:	1	"Management International Review", Pract
Citations:	18	Cites/author:	18.00	g-index:	1	Query date: 2016-01-08
Years:	3	Papers/author:	1.00	hI,norm:	1	Papers: 1 / Citations: 18
Cites/year:	6.00	Authors/paper:	1.00	hI,annual:	0.33	Years: 3

Cites		Per year	Rank	Authors	Title	Year	Publication
☑ h	18	6.00	1	AW Harzing	Practicing what we preach	2013	Management International Review

Second author's name is missing in master record

However, as Isabel Metz is not listed as an author, it does not show up when searching for her name. The reason for this is that Google Scholar has not parsed Isabel's name in the record that it has chosen as a master record (see screenshot).

Practicing what we preach
AW Harzing - Management International Review, 2013 - Springer
Abstract With the increasing globalisation of knowledge and management education, it is important that we build on our scanty understanding of trends and levels of geographic diversification in editorial board membership of management journals. Our study ...
Cited by 18   Related articles   Cite   Save

Practicing what We Preach
AW Harzing, I Metz - Management International Review - Springer
Abstract• With the increasing globalisation of knowledge and management education, it is important that we build on our scanty understanding of trends and levels of geographic diversification in editorial board membership of management journals.• Our study ...
Cite

Practicing what We Preach: The Geographic Diversity of Editorial Boards
AW Harzing, I Metz - Management international review, 2013 - cat.inist.fr
Résumé/Abstract With the increasing globalisation of knowledge and management education, it is important that we build on our scanty understanding of trends and levels of geographic diversification in editorial board membership of management journals. Our ...
Cite

In spite of linking to a correct publisher's version

This is a little puzzling as the master record links to a correct presentation of the article on the publisher's website (see screenshot) that includes Isabel's name.

Research Article

Management International Review

April 2013, Volume 53, Issue 2, pp 169-187

First online: 10 January 2012

Practicing what We Preach

The Geographic Diversity of Editorial Boards

Anne-Wil Harzing ✉ , Isabel Metz

Second and third version of the record have problems too

Interestingly, the name is correctly parsed in the second version of the record, but here the year is missing instead. The third version of the record provides all the correct details, but doesn't link to actual article itself. Sometimes you just can't win!

PoP tip 68: Google Scholar limitations (4):
Online listing as year of publication

These days the majority of publishers will make accepted articles available on their website well before they are published in print, using terms such as "online first", "early view" or "advance online publication". Unfortunately, this leads to some inconsistency in the way the publication is reported in Google Scholar and Publish or Perish.

Using online publication provides up-to-date research record

Especially in the Social Sciences, journals often have long backlogs and articles can be available online 6-24 months before they appear in print. Google Scholar parses articles as soon as they are available online (typically within a week of the article being listed) and can thus record both the publication and its citations to them well before they appear in print. Google Scholar thus presents a much more up to date record of an academic's research performance than for instance the Web of Science, which only enters publications after they have been published in print (and sometimes with substantive delays even then).

Difference in online and print publication year creates confusion

Unfortunately, this also creates some confusion as to **when** articles are published, as even when they have appeared in print, the publisher's website will normally list the online publication date as well [see below].

The impact of language barriers on trust formation in multinational teams

Helene Tenzer, Markus Pudelko & Anne-Wil Harzing

Affiliations | Corresponding author

Journal of International Business Studies (2014) 45, 508–535 | doi:10.1057/jibs.2013.64
Received 13 November 2012 | Revised 26 September 2013 | Accepted 16 October 2013 |
Published online 19 December 2013

Google Scholar does not parse publication years consistently

A problem arises when Google Scholar parses the online publication date as the publication year for some articles, but not others. For the journal above, we looked at all 19 articles that were included in the journal's 2013 h-index.

Cites	Per year	Authors	Title	Year	Publication
h 52	26.00	S Beugelsdijk, R Mudambi	MNEs as border-crossing multi-location enterpr...	2013	...International Business Studies
h 51	25.50	E Autio, S Pathak, K Wennberg	Consequences of cultural practices for entrepr...	2013	...of International Business
h 45	22.50	KD Brouthers	A retrospective on: Institutional, cultural and t...	2013	Journal of International Business...
h 41	20.50	S Ronen, O Shenkar	Mapping world cultures: Cluster formation, so...	2013	Journal of International Business...
h 41	20.50	ER Banalieva, C Dhanaraj	Home-region orientation in international expan...	2013	...International Business Studies
h 40	20.00	X Ma, TW Tong, M Fitza	How much does subnational region matter to f...	2013	Journal of International Business...
h 37	18.50	JM Shaver	Do we really need more entry mode studies&q...	2013	Journal of International Business...
h 36	18.00	A Goerzen, CG Asmussen	Global cities and multinational enterprise locati...	2013	...of International Business ...
h 34	17.00	H Tenzer, M Pudelko...	The impact of language barriers on trust form...	2013	...of International Business
h 32	16.00	N Boubakri, SA Mansi, W Saffar	Political institutions, connectedness, and corp...	2013	...of International Business ...
h 30	15.00	D Castellani, A Jimenez...	How remote are R&D labs [quest] Distance fac...	2013	...of International Business ...
h 25	12.50	JC Casillas...	Speed of the internationalization process: The...	2013	...of International Business ...
h 23	11.50	PJ Hinds, TB Neeley...	Language as a lightning rod: Power contests,...	2013	...of International Business ...
h 23	11.50	R Belderbos, B Leten, S Suzuki	How global is R&D [quest] Firm-level determin...	2013	...of International Business ...
h 23	11.50	G Qian, L Li, AM Rugman	Liability of country foreignness and liability of r...	2013	Journal of International Business...
h 21	10.50	Y Zeng, O Shenkar, SH Lee...	Cultural differences, MNE learning abilities, an...	2013	...of International Business ...
h 20	10.00	A Schmitt, J Van Biesebroeck	Proximity strategies in outsourcing relations: T...	2013	...of International Business ...
h 20	10.00	BR Chabowski, S Samiee...	A bibliometric analysis of the global branding lit...	2013	...of International Business ...
h 20	10.00	L Dai, L Eden, PW Beamish	Place, space, and geographical exposure: For...	2013	...International Business Studies

Out of all these articles, fourteen were in online first and published in the same year (2013), four were in online first in 2012, published in 2013, and parsed as 2013. This is as expected. However, two articles (Tenzer, Pudelko & Harzing, 2014 and Hinds, Neeley & Cramton, 2014) were in online first in 2013 (19 and 12 December respectively), published in 2014, but parsed as 2013.

Accurate record of journal publications in a particular year not possible

This is a little problematic as it means that one cannot get an accurate record of what is published in a particular journal in a particular year. At the same time one cannot simply compare online publication years either, as some articles have different online and print publication years in Google Scholar. As we saw above, four of the top 19 articles in 2013 were online in 2012. For 2014, the most cited article (Teece, 2014) was online in 2013, but was still parsed as 2014.

Authors cannot accurately compare the impact of their articles

This also creates problems for authors who want to compare citations to their paper with citations to other articles in the same journal in the same year. The 2014 Tenzer et al. and Hinds et al. papers – that were part of a special issue on language - compare well with 2013 papers (ranked 9th and 13th with 34 and 23 citations respectively), but if they had been compared to articles published in 2014, they would have ranked 2nd and 5th (see screen-shot below).

Now other articles in the special issue appear to be more highly cited on a cites per year basis. Chidow et al. for instance was published online on the 2nd of January, a mere two weeks after Tenzer et al., and thus is parsed as a 2014 article.

151

Cites		Per year	Authors	Title	Year	Publication
☑ h	74	74.00	DJ Teece	A dynamic capabilities-based entrepreneurial t...	2014	Journal of International Business...
☑ h	31	31.00	J Lu, X Liu, M Wright...	International experience and FDI location choi...	2014	... of International Business ...
☑ h	24	24.00	MY Brannen, R Piekkari...	The multifaceted role of language in internatio...	2014	... of International Business ...
☑ h	21	21.00	KE Meyer, Y Ding, J Li, H Zhang	Overcoming distrust: How state-owned enterp...	2014	... of International Business ...
☑ h	17	17.00	MH Li, L Cui, J Lu	Varieties in state capitalism: Outward FDI stra...	2014	Journal of International Business...
☑ h	17	17.00	A Cuervo-Cazurra, A Inkpen...	Governments as owners: State-owned multina...	2014	... Business Studies
☑ h	16	16.00	G Bekaert, CR Harvey, CT Lu...	Political risk spreads	2014	... Business Studies
☑ h	15	15.00	S Sui, M Baum	Internationalization strategy, firm resources a...	2014	Journal of International Business...
☑ h	14	14.00	A Chidlow, E Plakoyiannaki...	Translation in cross-language international bus...	2014	... of International Business ...
☑ h	14	14.00	H Liang, B Ren, SL Sun	An anatomy of state control in the globalizatio...	2014	Journal of International Business ...
☑ h	14	14.00	S Awate, MM Larsen...	Accessing vs sourcing knowledge: A comparati...	2014	... of International Business ...
☑ h	13	13.00	V Peltokorpi, E Vaara	Knowledge transfer in multinational corporatio...	2014	Journal of International Business ...

My recommendation for Google Scholar parsing

Ideally, we would want Google Scholar to parse a publication with its online publication year as soon as it is published, but revert to the in-print publication year once this is effective. This is indeed what Google Scholar seems to do for most, but unfortunately not all, publications.

Your notes

PoP tip 69: Google Scholar limitations (5): Stray citations

Stray citations

Google Scholar results (and thus Publish or Perish) often report multiple occurrences of the same publication. Please note that this is not the same as multiple web versions of the same paper as these are normally aggregated under one master record.

What we mean here are "stray citations" that have not been aggregated under the master record. These 2nd (and sometimes 3rd and further) versions typically only have a small number of citations each. Stray citations are generally the result of misspelling of an author's name, the title of the publication or the journal, or listing of the wrong volume, issue or page numbers. They can also occur through Google Scholar parsing errors.

Most stray citations are of the [citation] document type

Most stray citations are of the Google Scholar document type "[citation]". These are results to which Google Scholar found references, but for which the original work was not found online. However, the reverse is not necessarily true: not all results with a "[citation]" document type are stray citations.

Most books and book chapters, and non-print works such as software programs will have a "[citation]" document type. Two of my own more highly cited works – a research monograph and the Publish or Perish software - carry the [citation] document type.

[CITATION] Managing the multinationals: An international study of control mechanisms
AW Harzing - 1999 - E. Elgar
Cited by 380   Related articles   Cite   Save   More

[CITATION] Publish or perish
AW Harzing - 2007
Cited by 309   Related articles   Cite   Save

Publish or Perish features to deal with stray citations

Publish or Perish has two features that allow you to deal with stray citations.

- First, you can use the **Uncheck CITATION** button, which deselects all [citation] records and removes them from the citation metrics.
- Second, if you consider the stray citations to be valid, you can merge them simply by dragging them onto the master record.

Stray citations in the Web of Science

It is important to note that stray citations are not unique to Google Scholar. They are prevalent in the Web of Science as well if you use the "Cited Reference" search [which includes references to books and non-ISI listed journals] rather than the general search function.

- Culture's consequences: a highly cited book

One of the most-cited academics in the field of Management – Geert Hofstede – has published a book called *"Culture's Consequences"*. This book was first published in 1980, with a 2nd revised edition in 2001. These two versions respectively have more than 8700 and more than 5500 citations under the title *"Cultures Consequence"*.

- More than 100 stray citation records for Culture's consequences

However, there are also more than 100 additional stray citation records in ISI's Cited Reference search, all referring to the same two books. Some of these entries refer to specific page numbers in the book and hence have been entered as separate entries. Others refer inaccurately to different publication years or misrepresent the book's title as *"Cultural Consequences"*.

- Weird title variations probably caused by data entry errors

Many stray entries in ISI are simple misspellings of the title, with some of the weirdest being "CULTURES CIONSEQUENC", "CULTUES UCULTURES CO", and "CULTURES OCNSEQUENCE". In many of these cases, the references were actually correct in the referring works and the spelling errors appear to have been made by ISI data entry staff. Most of these inaccurate references only occur once or twice, but a substantial number has a double-digit number of citations, with three accumulating more than 50 citations.

- In fact Google Scholar does a better job than WoS with stray citations

Ironically, none of the more than 14000 citations to this work was presented correctly, as its title is *"Culture's Consequences"*, not *"Cultures Consequence"*. The reason for the wrong tile is that the Web of Science does not seem to be able to deal with apostrophes and has a fixed 20-character length for the Cited Work record. In contrast, Google Scholar has less than 30 variations of this title. Hence Google Scholar's aggregation mechanism might actually be better than the Web of Science!

PoP tip 70: Google Scholar limitations (6): All citations attributed to the last edition of a book

Three editions of a textbook

Many books, including academic textbooks, but also successful research monographs, go through several editions. Below is the third edition of my IHRM textbook. The first edition was published in 1995, the second in 2004. [Google Scholar does not seem to have picked up the 4th edition (2014) yet.]

[BOOK] International human resource management

AW Harzing, A Pinnington - 2010 - books.google.com
The eagerly-awaited Third Edition of the hugely successful International Human Resource Management succeeds in maintaining the academic rigour and critical focus that have established its reputation as the most authoritative and cutting-edge text in the field. ...
Cited by 346   Related articles   All 15 versions   Cite   Save   More

Citing works predating the cited work

342 cites is quite a respectable number of citations for such a young book, but if we look at the citing works, we understand why. Many of the citing works date from well before 2010. In fact, only about 100 citations dated from 2011 onwards.

☑ *h*	349	16.62	AWK Harzing	The persistent myth of high expatriate fai...	1995
☑ *h*	72	3.60	N Forster, M Johnsen	Expatriate management policies in UK com...	1996
☑ *h*	60	3.00	R Verburg	Developing HRM in foreign-Chinese joint v...	1996
☑	20	1.00	ED Honeycutt Jr, JB Ford	Potential problems and solutions when hiri...	1996
☑ *h*	56	2.95	JP Begin	Dynamic human resource systems: Cross-...	1997
☑	28	1.47	C Brewster	International HRM: beyond expatriation	1997
☑	21	1.11	S Frey-Ridgway	The cultural dimension of international bu...	1997

All cites aggregated to latest edition leading to high cites/year value

Google Scholar simply aggregates all citations to a book to its latest edition. So if a book has multiple editions with the same title, all citations will be attributed to its latest edition. As a result these books usually have very high citation per year rates and end up being at the top of the ranking for most academics when you sort on the **[cites] per year** column.

PoP tip 71: Google Scholar limitations (7): Removal of subject areas

In the early days, Google Scholar provided the opportunity to filter by subject area (see screenshot).

- ✓ Biology, Life Sciences, Environmental Science
- ✓ Business, Administration, Finance, Economics
- ✓ Chemistry and Materials Science
- ✓ Engineering, Computer Science, Mathematics
- ✓ Medicine, Pharmacology, Veterinary Science
- ✓ Physics, Astronomy, Planetary Science
- ✓ Social Sciences, Arts, Humanities

Subject area classification was not flawless

This feature wasn't flawless; some journals (and thus an author's publications in those journals) were classified in clearly inappropriate disciplines. Some articles appeared not to be classified at all, and were only shown if all subject categories were ticked. However, this feature was VERY useful when searching for authors with a very common name as it allowed you to distinguish Peter Smith the physicist from Peter Smith the archaeologist, and Peter Smith the computer scientist.

Google Scholar removed subject areas in May 2012

Unfortunately, in May 2012 Google Scholar redesigned its interface and integrated the advanced search page in its general search page. In doing so, it removed the option to select specific subject areas. As a result subject area filtering is now no longer possible, neither in Google Scholar, nor in Publish or Perish.

For more information see:

> http://googlescholar.blogspot.com.au/2012/05/our-new-modern-look.html

If you would like to see subject areas reinstated, let Google Scholar know. Obviously, there is no guarantee they will listen, but we can always try...

> http://support.google.com/scholar/bin/request.py?contact_type=general

PoP tip 72: Google Scholar limitations (8): You can only restrict publication years, not citation years

Many Publish or Perish users would like to know how many citations they received in say the last year or the last five years and expect the year limitations in Publish or Perish to achieve this.

- For instance: You have just done a search (any search) with specific start and end years, for example from 2000 to 2005. However, the results do not show "6 years active" as you expected, but "10 years active" (if the search is done in 2009). What's going on?
- Answer: The search period (2000 to 2005 in the example) restricts the **original publications**. It does not restrict the **citations**.

Citations are always shown until the present day

Regardless of the start and end years in your query, the results will always show the citations until the present day, give or take a few weeks. And because Publish or Perish shows citation statistics, we must count all years from the start year until the present day.

Classifying citing works by year

Theoretically, you could review all citations to your work and classify them by year. However, this would require many additional queries to Google Scholar, which will likely lead to very slow searches and CAPTCHAs

The alternative: use Google Scholar Citations

If you have created a Google Scholar Citations profile you can get a nice graph indicating your citations over the years (see below).

Citation indices	All	Since 2011
Citations	9442	5694
h-index	45	40
i10-index	82	70

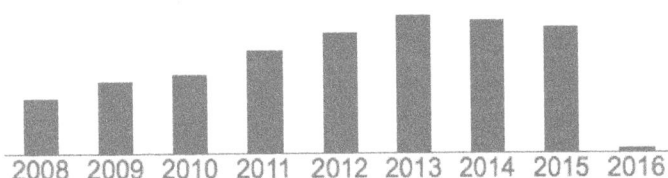

2008 2009 2010 2011 2012 2013 2014 2015 2016

PoP tip 73: Google Scholar limitations (9): Slow searches

Many academics that have been using Publish or Perish for a while have noticed that searches are now slower than they were in the past. This is to avoid exceeding the maximum acceptable Google Scholar request rate.

Number of results per page 20 (down from 100)

In February 2013 Google Scholar reduced the maximum number of results per page from 100 to 20. This means that Publish or Perish now has to retrieve up to 5 times as many result pages per query in order to show the full results.

- More page requests mean that Publish or Perish hits the maximum number of requests that Google Scholar allows per hour sooner.
- If the number of page requests exceeds the maximum that Google Scholar allows, Google Scholar will temporarily block your IP address. This block can last 1-2 days.
- To avoid hitting the maximum allowable request limit, Publish or Perish now uses an adaptive request rate limiter. This limits the number of requests that are sent to Google Scholar within a given period, both short-term (during the last 60 seconds) and medium term (during the last hour).
- To achieve the required reduction in requests, Publish or Perish delays subsequent requests for a variable amount of time (up to 1 minute). The higher the recent request rate, the longer the delays.

Net results: queries take longer than before

The net result is that queries will take longer than before. The alternative is being blocked by Google Scholar. We consider the relatively short delays during queries as the lesser evil; hence the adaptive rate limiter.

No effects for occasional search

If you perform queries with few results or only search occasionally, then the request rate limiter will have little or no effect on the query time. In this case, the required delays are short or non-existent, and Publish or Perish will retrieve result pages as fast as it did in the past.

Longer delays for queries with many results or done in short succession

However, if you perform queries that yield many results (several hundred or more) or issue a number of queries in short succession, then the request rate limiter will insert progressively longer delays to keep the overall request rate within acceptable limits. If you want to avoid this, then the best remedy is to spread your queries over the day.

PoP tip 74: Google Scholar limitations (10): CAPTCHAS

Publish or Perish is doing everything to limit burdening Google Scholar with too many queries.

- We keep results in the cache, so there is no need to query Google Scholar if you run the same search repeatedly within a short period.
- We limit the request rate so that if you perform queries that yield many results (several hundred or more) or issue a number of queries in short succession, the request rate limiter will insert progressively longer delays to keep the overall request rate within acceptable limits.
- We alert you if your request rate is running too high.

CAPTCHAS are unavoidable at very high request rates

Please show you're not a robot

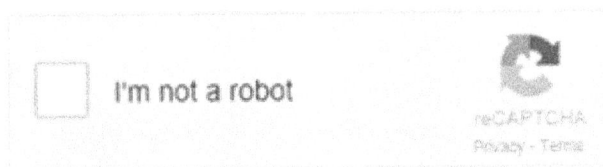

I'm not a robot

reCAPTCHA
Privacy - Terms

How to "solve" captchas

After clicking the box, you will be presented with either a range of images from which you need to select a specific type of image or a squiggly word that you need to type into a box. Once you have identified the correct images (usually street signs, oceans, boats, homes, cars, food etc.), you will normally get a second set of images. If you identify both sets correctly, your search will proceed as normal.

How to prevent captchas

We realise this is very annoying, but there is really nothing we can do about this. You can avoid this by not running too many queries in a short space of time and being smart in your queries so that you do not get hundreds of irrelevant results.

.

Your notes

PoP tip 75: Using PoP (1): The buttons

Now you know what functions can be performed with Publish or Perish, maybe you can spend a bit of time getting to get to know the features of the PoP interface a little better? This will ensure you get the best out of the software.

Top-right hand buttons

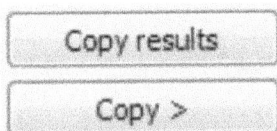

Let's look at the buttons first. At the top right-hand you will find four buttons. You have already used lookup and maybe lookup Direct, but what is the difference?

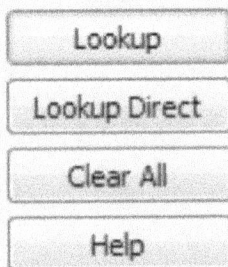

- **Lookup** Looks up the current query, using the internal cache if possible. This means that if you have run the query before, the results will come from the cache and the search is not submitted to Google Scholar again. This is quicker and does not create unnecessary strain on Google Scholar.
- **Lookup Direct** Looks up the current query, bypassing the internal cache and contacting Google Scholar directly. Only use Lookup Direct if you really want "fresh" data.
- **Clear All** simply clears anything you have entered into the search boxes. Useful if you want to start with a clean slate.
- **Help**, surprise surprise ... takes you to the help file.

Right hand buttons

The second set of buttons is divided into four sets. The first set of copy buttons allow you to very quickly copy data from PoP to other programs.

- **Copy results**: Click this button to copy all currently selected results plus the corresponding metrics to the Windows clipboard. You can then paste them into another application. The keyboard shortcut for this command is **Ctrl+Shift+C**.
- The next button (**Copy >**) unfolds another drop-down menu, allowing you to export either the statistics (the upper part of the results with all the metrics) or the list of publications with their details. You can chose three different formats, depending on your needs and for the CSV and Excel format can export with or without header.

Please note: If you want copy data from several queries at once, use the popup menu commands from the multi-query center's list view.

Copy Statistics as Text
Copy Statistics as CSV
Copy Statistics as CSV with Header
Copy Statistics for Excel
Copy Statistics for Excel with Header

Copy Results as Text
Copy Results as CSV
Copy Results as CSV with Header
Copy Results for Excel
Copy Results for Excel with Header

Copy [...] for Excel with Header most useful

I normally find the **Excel with Header** most useful. After you paste to Excel, it shows you the data in a nice column format that you can then convert to a sortable table with just one click [Use **Insert Table** in Excel].

Statistics

Query	Papers	Citations	Years	Cites_Per Year	Cites_Paper	Cites_Author	Papers_Author	Authors_Paper	h_index
a harzing: all	111	9497	20	474.9	85.56	7043.05	73.15	1.86	45

Publications

Cites	Authors	Title	Year	Source
474	AW Harzing	Publish or perish	2007	
472	AW Harzing	Acquisitions versus greenfield investments: International strateg	2002	Strategic management journal
436	NJ Adler, AW Harzing	When knowledge wins: Transcending the sense and nonsense o	2009	Academy of Management Learning & ...
435	AW Harzing	An empirical analysis and extension of the Bartlett and Ghoshal	2000	Journal of international business studies
409	AW Harzing	Managing the multinationals: An international study of control r	1999	
371	AW Harzing, R Van der Wal	Google Scholar: the democratization of citation analysis	2007	Ethics in science and environmental ...
347	AWK Harzing	The persistent myth of high expatriate failure rates	1995	International Journal of Human Resource
341	AW Harzing, A Pinnington	International human resource management	2010	
337	AW Harzing	Of bears, bumble-bees, and spiders: The role of expatriates in co	2002	Journal of World Business
321	AW Harzing	Response rates in international mail surveys: Results of a 22-cou	1997	International Business Review
280	AW Harzing, A Sorge	The relative impact of country of origin and universal contingeni	2003	Organization Studies
263	AW Harzing	Response Styles in Cross-national Survey Research A 26-country	2006	International Journal of Cross Cultural ...
261	AW Harzing	Who's in charge? An empirical study of executive staffing practic	2001	Human Resource Management
242	AJ Feely, AW Harzing	Language management in multinational companies	2003	Cross Cultural Management: An ...

Check and uncheck buttons

The second and third sets of buttons allow you to check or uncheck either **all** publications or a **sub-set** of them

- those that have 0 citations
- those that are of the [citation] format. These are results to which Google Scholar found references, but for which the original work was not found online.
- any other selection that you have made. You can select publications with the keyboard or mouse, in the same way you would in most programs.

The final button simply repeats the help button and takes you to that part of the help file that is relevant to the lower panel.

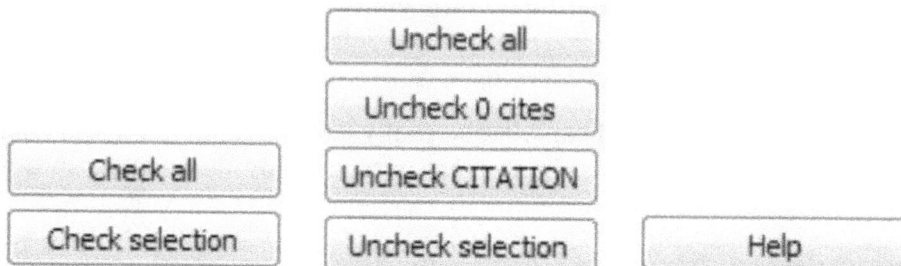

Uncheck all

Uncheck 0 cites

Check all   Uncheck CITATION

Check selection   Uncheck selection   Help

PoP tip 76: Using PoP (2): Resizing and sorting columns

The columns in the results area can be resized to your preference by dragging the lines between them, and will stay that way until you resize them again. Hence you can decide which fields you want to see in full and which are less important.

Reorganizing the display by making columns disappear

You can also make columns "disappear" by making them really small. So if you don't need the "rank" column (which indicates the order in which the results were ordered in Google Scholar) between the per year and author column, just make it disappear. If for whatever reason you'd like to compare total citations and citations per year directly with the year and journal outlet, just make the author and title field disappear.

Cites	Per year	Year	Publication
☑ h 453	34.85	2002	Strategic management journal
☑ h 443	73.83	2009	Academy of Management Learning & ...
☑ h 436	29.07	2000	Journal of international business studies
☑ h 382	23.88	1999	
☑ h 373	46.63	2007	Ethics in science and environmental ...
☑ h 348	17.40	1995	International Journal of Human Resource ...
☑ h 344	26.46	2002	Journal of World Business

Sorting the results by clicking on the column heading

You can also sort the results on any column by clicking on the column heading and sort them the other way around by clicking again. As default the results are sorted by decreasing citations. However, you might want to sort by [citations] **per year** to see which of your papers have had the biggest impact on a yearly basis.

Sorting on [cites] per year identifies papers with high citation potential

As you can see below some of my 2013 papers (#6 and #12) look like they might become highly cited over the years even though their current citation levels are still modest. You would not be able to spot this as easily when sorting by total citations.

Sorting on author, title, or publication helps with merging or author disambiguation

Sorting by author, title, or publication (source) can also be really useful when you are trying to merge stray citations or when you are devising a strategy to exclude namesakes in another field.

Cites			Per year	Authors	Title
☑	*h*	438	73.00	NJ Adler, AW Harzing	When knowledge wins: Transcending the sense and no...
☑	*h*	446	55.75	AW Harzing	Publish or perish
☑	*h*	369	46.13	AW Harzing, R Van d...	Google Scholar: the democratization of citation analysis
☑	*h*	450	34.62	AW Harzing	Acquisitions versus greenfield investments: Internation...
☑	*h*	196	32.67	N Noorderhaven, AW...	Knowledge-sharing and social interaction within MNEs
☑	*h*	163	32.60	AW Harzing	The publish or perish book
☑	*h*	64	32.00	AW Harzing	A preliminary test of Google Scholar as a source for cita...
☑	*h*	183	30.50	AW Harzing, R Van D...	A Google Scholar h-index for journals: An alternative m...
☑	*h*	266	29.56	AW Harzing	Response Styles in Cross-national Survey Research A 2...
☑	*h*	435	29.00	AW Harzing	An empirical analysis and extension of the Bartlett and ...
☑	*h*	338	26.00	AW Harzing	Of bears, bumble-bees, and spiders: The role of expatr...
☑	*h*	181	25.86	AW Harzing, AJ Feely	The language barrier and its implications for HQ-subsidi...
☑	*h*	51	25.50	AW Harzing, M Pudelko	Language competencies, policies and practices in multin...

PoP tip 77: Using PoP (3): Context menu

If you right-click on any result in the Publish or Perish list of publications, you will get a contextual menu (see screenshot). Of this menu, we have already discussed all copy and check/uncheck commands as they also appear as buttons.

We have discussed the **Save as ...** and **Export to Archive ...** commands in separate tips on importing, exporting and archiving your data.

Results

Papers:	207	Cites/paper:	46.31	h-index:		Split Citations
Citations:	9587	Cites/author:	7104.82	g-index:		Recalculate Metrics
Years:	20	Papers/author:	148.35	hI,norm:		
Cites/year:	479.35	Authors/paper:	1.75	hI,annual:		Open Article in Browser

Context menu items:
- Open Article in Browser
- Open Citations/Related in Browser
- Lookup Citations
- Copy Statistics as Text
- Copy Statistics as CSV
- Copy Statistics as CSV with Header
- Copy Statistics for Excel
- Copy Statistics for Excel with Header
- Copy Results as Text — Ctrl+Shift+C
- Copy Results as CSV
- Copy Results as CSV with Header
- Copy Results for Excel
- Copy Results for Excel with Header
- Check/Select All — Ctrl+A
- Check Selection — Num +
- Uncheck All — Ctrl+U
- Uncheck 0 Cites — Ctrl+0
- Uncheck Selection — Num -
- Save As BibTeX...
- Save As CSV... — Ctrl+S
- Save As EndNote... — Ctrl+Shift+S
- Save As ISI Export...
- Save As RefMan/RIS...
- Export to Archive...

Cites	Per year	Authors	Title
☑ h 450	34.62	AW Harzing	Acquisitions versus greenfie
☑ h 446	55.75	AW Harzing	Publish or perish
☑ h 438	73.00	NJ Adler, AW H...	When knowledge wins: Tra
☑ h 435	29.00	AW Harzing	An empirical analysis and ex
☑ h 374	23.38	AW Harzing	Managing the multinationals
☑ h 369	46.13	AW Harzing, R ...	Google Scholar: the democra
☑ h 345	17.25	AWK Harzing	The persistent myth of high
☑ h 341	56.83	AW Harzing, A ...	International human resour
☑ h 338	26.00	AW Harzing	Of bears, bumble-bees, and
☑ h 321	17.83	AW Harzing	Response rates in internatio
☑ h 280	23.33	AW Harzing, A ...	The relative impact of count
☑ h 266	29.56	AW Harzing	Response Styles in Cross-na
☑ h 259	18.50	AW Harzing	Who's in charge? An empiric
☑ h 243	20.25	AJ Feely, AW H...	Language management in m
☑ h 196	32.67	N Noorderhave...	Knowledge-sharing and soc
☑ h 183	30.50	AW Harzing, R ...	A Google Scholar h-index fo
☑ h 183	22.88	M Pudelko, AW ...	Country-of-origin, localizati
☑ h 181	25.86	AW Harzing, AJ...	The language barrier and its
☑ h 175	14.58	AW Harzing	The role of culture in entry
☑ h 174	11.60	AW Harzing	Cross-national industrial ma
☑ h 163	32.60	AW Harzing	The publish or perish book
☑ h 154	11.85	AW Harzing	Are our referencing errors u
☑ h 146	10.43	AW Harzing	An analysis of the functions
☑ h 138	12.55	J Barry Hocking...	A knowledge transfer persp
☑ h 128	11.64	AW Harzing, C ...	Expatriate failure: time to a
☑ h 123	13.67	AW Harzing, N ...	Knowledge flows in MNCs: A
☑ h 116	14.50	J Mingers, AW ...	Ranking journals in business
☑ h 99	9.00	B Myloni, AWK ...	Host country specific factor

0/0 rpm   0/10m   0/h   2/4h   44587 total

Context menu command options

So that leaves us with the first four commands:

- **Open Article in Browser**. Opens the currently selected article in your web browser. This command is only available for some items (depending on the information that Google Scholar provided) and may sometimes open the abstract rather than the full article.

- **Open Citations/Related in Browser**. Opens the Google Scholar web page that lists the referencing articles for the current item, if available. In absence of that, opens the Google Scholar "related" web page, if available.

- **Lookup Citations**. Looks up the citing works for the currently selected results in a separate PoP query [see Tip 53].

- **Split Citations**: Is only active if you have merged publications. You use it when you have accidentally merged the wrong publications.

PoP tip 78: Using PoP (4): Top and left-hand menu

File   Edit   Query   View   Tools   Help

Now we are talking about menus, please have a browse through the menu at the top. Here you can access all the menu options we have discussed so far, plus a few more. Just explore a little!

Citation analysis

Author impact

Journal impact

General citations

Multi-query center

Publish or Perish tips

PoP tips overview

Tips: Author search

Tips: Journal search

Tips: General search

Tips: Multi-query center

Tips: ISI data import

Tips: Scopus data import

Help resources

Help contents

2-Minute intro

PoP FAQ

PoP web site

PoP book

Take online survey

Program maintenance

Check for updates

What's new?

Web browser

The left-hand menu has four major sections:

Citation analysis

Allows you to move between the different options for citation analysis:

- Author impact: search for your own or someone else's citation metrics
- Journal impact: searches in which the journal takes centre stage
- General search: sophisticated searches for the more advanced user

You can also go directly to the multi-query center, which stores all your queries and allows for sophisticated query management.

Publish or Perish tips

This section gives you direct access to the most important Publish or Perish tips. Please use it whenever you have any questions or even before to ensure you search in the most effective way.

Help resources

This section directs you to all available help resources. Even if you don't want to read software helpfiles or FAQs, please at least look at the 2-minute intro!

Program maintenance

This section allows you to check for updates to ensure you are using the latest version of Publish or Perish.

It also links to a "What's new?" which will tell you what changed if you have just updated your PoP version.

The web browser provides access to the Web without having to leave Publish or Perish.

Please use the available help resources and tips

Interestingly, and somewhat annoyingly, I get many emails with requests for help from academics who are highly surprised there is a help file. There really is one! There are links called **Help** in the left-hand column, the right-hand column, and the top-menu. Clicking on the question mark at the top right hand corner gets you context sensitive help.

Some users have been running sub-optimal queries for years, wasting many hours of their time. Using the available help resources will make your searches much more effective. If I got a pound for everyone who said: Sorry, I didn't know there was a ... [fill the blank]: help-file, FAQ, Book, Website, Journal impact search, Keyword search, Multi-query center, I would be a rich woman ;-)

PoP tip 79: Setting preferences: General preferences

This dialog box appears when you choose the **Tools > Preferences** command from the Publish or Perish main menu. Unless you know what you are doing, don't change any of these preferences. The default settings are chosen to ensure the best result for nearly all users.

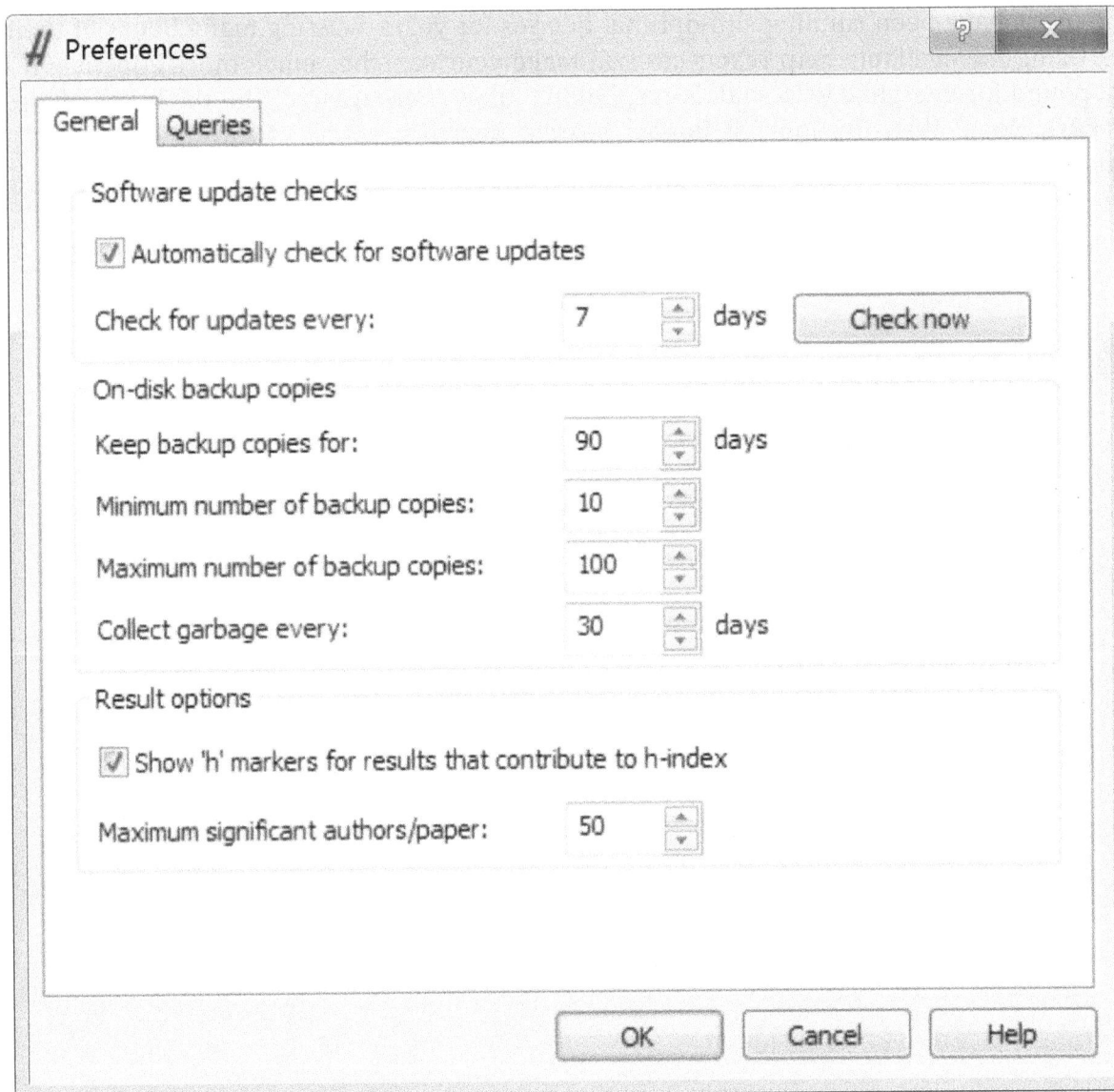

The general preferences allow you to edit a number of settings that affect Publish or Perish as a whole. This dialog box contains the following fields and options.

Software update checks

This box contains options relating to the periodic checks that the Publish or Perish software performs to inform you about available updates to the software. If an update is available, you will be prompted to download and install it.

On-disk backup copies

This box contains options relating to the on-disk backup copies that Publish or Perish makes of your queries and their results. These copies are meant as an insurance against catastrophic failures of the system or in the Publish or Perish software (for example, a power outage just when Publish or Perish is saving its query results). You do not really need to understand these options. Publish or Perish will automatically ask you to restore data when you restart after unexpected termination of the program. If you do want to know more, check the help file.

Result options

This box contains options that affect the way Publish or Perish calculates and displays its results.

Show 'h' markers for results that contribute to the h-index

Check this box to let Publish or Perish display a small 'h' icon in front of all result items that contribute to the h-index; clear it to omit the icon. The 'h' icon makes it easier to identify which result items are part of the h-index and which items are not, and must therefore gain additional citations to increase the h-index.

Maximum significant authors/paper

Enter the maximum number of authors per paper that PoP will use to calculate metrics. This affects only metrics that take the number of authors per paper into account (for example, the individual h-index). It is meant to cap the effects of excessively large numbers of authors per paper (i.e., more than a few dozen). After changing this value, you must manually trigger a recalculation of the affected metrics by choosing the **Recalculate Metrics** command from the Edit menu or from the context (pop-up) menu for the query in the multi-query center.

PoP tip 80: Setting preferences: Query preferences

This dialog box appears when you choose the **Tools > Preferences** command from the Publish or Perish main menu. Unless you know what you are doing, don't change any of these preferences. The default settings are chosen to ensure the best result for nearly all users.

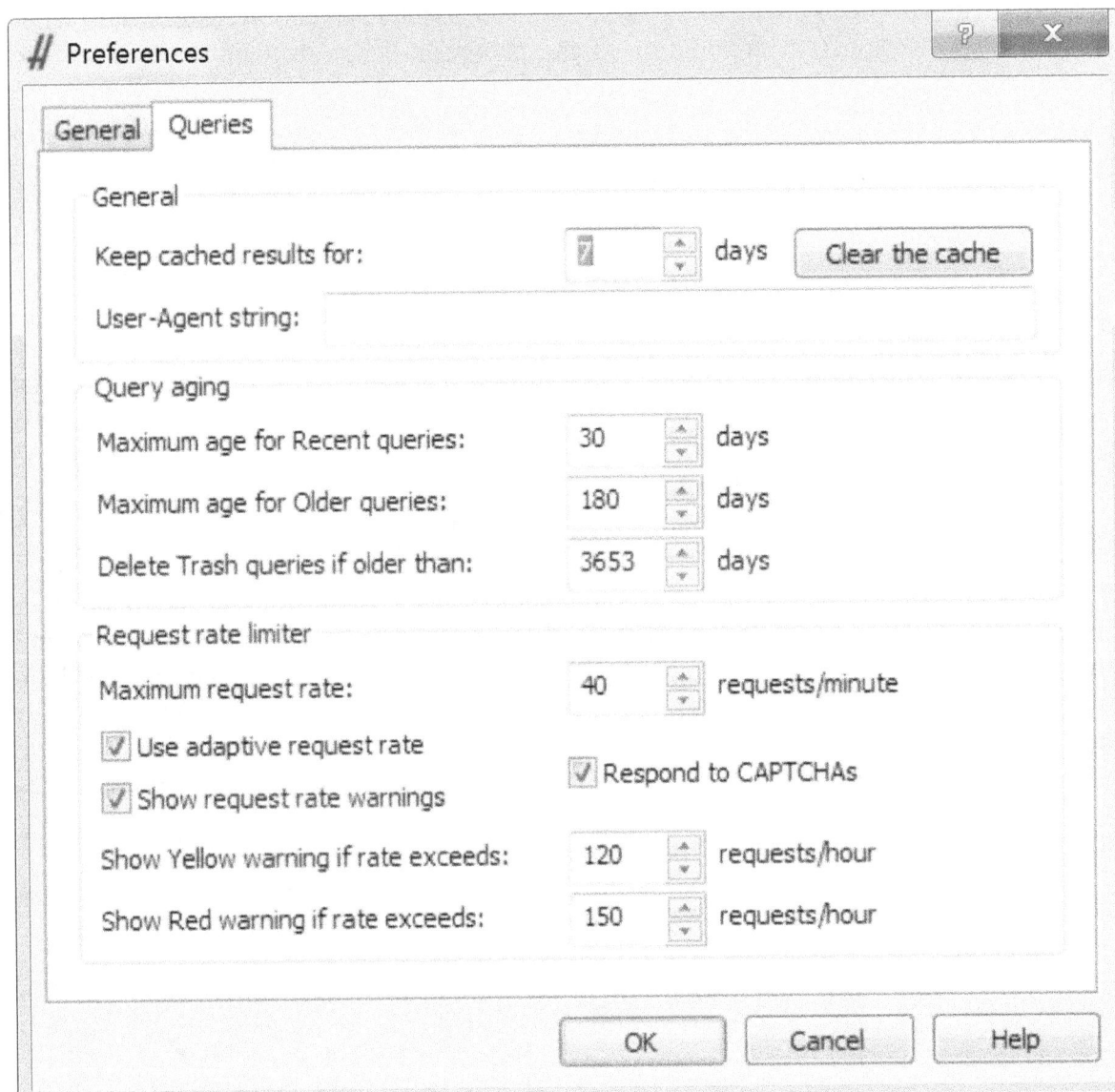

The query preferences allow you to edit a number of settings that affect how Publish or Perish handles queries. This dialog box contains the following fields and options.

General

- **Keep cached results for**: Enter the number of days to keep the query results from queries. The longer this period, the fewer accesses are required to satisfy repeated queries. Any updates in the query results only become visible after the cache period has expired, so you don't want to make this period too long.

- **Clear the cache**: Click this button to clear the entire results cache. This forces subsequent queries to access Google Scholar directly, which might be useful after a (suspected) update on Google Scholar, or if you have reason to believe that the cached results are somehow invalid.

- **User-Agent string**: 99.99% of the PoP users do not need to know what this means and there is no need to put anything in this box. If you think you do need to know more, have a look at the help file.

Query aging

This box contains options that determine how Publish or Perish ages previously executed queries. The aging of queries *only* applies to queries that reside in the **Recent queries**, **Older queries**, or **Trash** folders. Queries that reside in other folders of the Multi-query center are not affected by the aging policies.

Request rate limiter

This box contains options that determine how Publish or Perish limits the rate at which your requests are send to Google Scholar. If you sent too many requests to Google Scholar or if the requests follow each other too quickly, Google Scholar may block further requests. The request rate limiter options help you to keep the number of requests sent to Google Scholar down to acceptable levels.

Respond to CAPTCHAs

Check this box to display a CAPTCHA dialog box when Google Scholar requests verification of your human status. If you solve the CAPTCHA correctly, then Google Scholar allows further queries. We recommend that you leave this option checked.

Allow cookies in Internet Explorer settings

For the CAPTCHA handling to be functional, you must allow first-party cookies in your Internet Explorer settings, or at least session cookies. You can set the Internet Explorer cookies preferences by choosing the **Tools > Internet Options** command from the main menu in Publish or Perish, then clicking on the **Privacy** tab in the **Internet Properties** dialog box that appears.

173